*Tying and Fishing*
# TAILWATER FLIES

*Tying and Fishing*
# TAILWATER FLIES

## PAT DORSEY

HEADWATER
BOOKS

STACKPOLE
BOOKS

Copyright © 2010 by Stackpole Books

Published by
STACKPOLE BOOKS
Headwater Books
5067 Ritter Road
Mechanicsburg, PA 17055
www.stackpolebooks.com

Printed in China

First edition

Illustrations by Dave Hall

10  9  8  7  6  5  4  3  2  1

**Library of Congress Cataloging-in-Publication Data**

Dorsey, Pat, 1963–
   Tying and fishing tailwater flies / Pat Dorsey ; [Illustrations by Dave Hall]. — 1st ed.
      p. cm.
   Includes index.
   ISBN-13: 978-0-8117-0722-0 (hardcover)
   ISBN-10: 0-8117-0722-9 (hardcover)
   1. Fly tying. 2. Fly fishing. I. Title.
   SH451.D67 2010
   688.7'9124—dc22

                                               2010004635

*To my great uncle Jim Cantrall.*
*Thanks for teaching me how to tie my first fly.*
*Your passion for fly fishing and fly tying was contagious.*

# CONTENTS

# ACKNOWLEDGMENTS

I've been blessed with the opportunity to work with some of the best fly fishers, fly tiers, outdoor writers, and guides in the Rocky Mountain region who have all shared with me advice, flies, tricks, tips, techniques, and other nuances that have helped me become a better angler, tier, and guide. I'd like to thank the following influential industry professionals that I'm proud to call my friends—Bob Saile, Charlie Meyers, Ed Dentry, Ed Rolka, Scott Ratcliff, Jim Pruett, Randy Smith, Matt Miles, Harold Tygart, Ed Engle, John Barr, Jack Dennis, Charlie Craven, Landon Mayer, Shane Stalcup, Don Puterbaugh, Bob Dye, Jim Cannon, Monroe Coleman, Kevin Gregory, John Perizzolo, Steve Parrott, Jonathan Keisling, Clay Anselmo, Chris Wells, Eric Atha, Roger Bittell, Rich Pilatzke, John Smith, J. Core, John Keefover, Cody Scott, Kerry Caraghar, and Dave Opie. You are all valued streamside companions, and I appreciate your camaraderie both on and off the water.

My deepest appreciation goes out to John Barr who initiated my first conversation with Bruce Olson, new fly manager at Umpqua Feather Merchants, which led me to join the Signature Fly Designer Program for the best fly manufacturer in the world. Becoming a royalty tier for Umpqua was always a dream of mine—thanks for making it all possible. Special thanks also go to Jeff Fryhover, president of Umpqua Feather Merchants, and Brian Schmidt, fly production specialist, for their continued support.

I would like to also thank Van Rollo, one of the premier western reps and owner of Mountain Sports in Boulder, Colorado, for selling my flies to specialty fly shops throughout the Rocky Mountain region. Additionally, I would like to thank all the fly-shop owners who have purchased my flies and all those anglers who have fished my patterns with confidence.

I would also like to thank Jim and Martha Cannon for giving me an opportunity to pursue a livelihood in the fly-fishing industry. You are two of the most amazing and unselfish people I know—thanks for always being there, through thick and thin, and supporting all my fly-fishing endeavors. Thank you John Randolph and Ross Purnell of *Fly Fisherman* for your unending support. It has been a pleasure writing for the best fly-fishing publication in America. You have provided me with an avenue to share my passion for fly tying and fly fishing. Thanks for having faith and confidence in my writing.

Most importantly, none of this would be possible without the support of my family. Book projects tend to take on a life of their own, requiring the utmost patience from your loved ones. My wife, Kim Dorsey, has made tremendous sacrifices so that I could pursue my career and is one of the most incredible people I know. Thanks for your support, encouragement, and continued help at speaking engagements, trade shows, fly-tying seminars, and other events. We've been blessed with five wonderful children—Forrest, Zach, Hunter, Michael, and Nicole—who have also been supportive of my fly-fishing addiction.

In closing, I would like to especially thank Jay Nichols for his streamside companionship, encouragement, beautiful photos, guidance, photo coaching, and all the hours of editing this book to make it clear and concise.

# INTRODUCTION

I caught my first trout with my dad, Jim Dorsey, on the East River near Almont, Colorado, when I was ten. I remember that experience like it was yesterday—Dad and I tromped through a dense stand of mosquito-infested willows that eventually funneled into a prime run downstream from the Roaring Judy Fish Hatchery. The East River is a classic cottonwood-lined freestone river loaded with 12-inch brown trout. Fishing was good that day; in fact, that adventure changed my life forever. My first few trout ignited an undying love for fly fishing and the outdoors, which ultimately led to a livelihood in the fly-fishing industry.

Shortly after my first trip to the river, my great uncle Jim Cantrall showed me how to tie a few of his favorite patterns, such as the Swayback Ant, Gray Hackle Peacock, and Gray Hackle Yellow. The Swayback Ant (invented by the caretaker of the Swayback Ranch in Trumbull, Colorado) was an incredible fly at Cheesman Canyon and Deckers, and the Gray Hackle Yellow and Gray Hackle Peacock were excellent producers on both lakes and rivers such as the Colorado, Blue, Roaring Fork, and Eagle. I caught my first trout on one of Uncle Jim's Gray Hackle Yellows.

After my initial fly-tying lesson, Dad took me down to Anglers All, and we purchased a fly-tying kit from money that I saved from cutting the neighbor's lawn. A mow and trim back then was $4—that pretty well shot my life savings. Looking back at it now, that money may have been the best investment

*Fishing the Gunnison valley brings back vivid memories of the first few trout that I caught with my father, Jim Dorsey, nearly 35 years ago. Those memories are rekindled each time I set foot on the fabled Gunnison River.* JAY NICHOLS

*I have tied flies commercially for over twenty-five years. This book contains a lot of the tricks I have learned for speed and consistency.* JAY NICHOLS

of my life. My first kit had all the basic essentials: Thompson Model A vise, Solingen scissors, threader, hackle pliers, bobbin, Thompson whip-finisher, hair stacker, thread, copper and gold wire, Mustad hooks, head cement, marabou, peacock herl, pheasant feathers, a small patch of deer and elk hair, a brown Indian neck, black saddle hackle, chenille, and a basic assortment of dubbing. My biggest problem was that I didn't know how to use most of it.

Once my neighbor Brian Phillips (who was an avid fly fisherman) heard that I was beginning to tie flies, he let me borrow his copy of Jack Dennis' *Western Trout Fly Tying Manual, Volume 1*. Like many other self-taught tiers, my addiction was fueled by these manuals. I carefully studied the text and step-by-step tutorials and began tying everything from Hare's-Ear Nymphs to Adams dry flies.

It wasn't long before I had to replenish the materials that came with the original kit. I replaced them, and then some. I eventually set up my fly-tying room in the basement of my parents' home. I got my hands on a couple of old file cabinets and hung a piece of pegboard on the wall to hang all my materials from. Early on, I found good organization to be a key ingredient for successful fly tying.

Like many other tiers, I quickly figured out that you do not save money by tying your own flies. Don't get me wrong, there are many benefits to tying your own flies—but from a financial standpoint it's a losing proposition, especially when tying dry flies. During the winter when many trout streams are jammed with ice and you cannot fish, tying flies helps you overcome the winter doldrums and lifts your spirit. I use this downtime to organize and replenish my fly boxes for the upcoming season. Tying flies is also immensely satisfying. I am an amateur entomologist, but when I am able to match the hatch with a replica that I have tied and bring a trout to net that took my pattern as it would have taken a natural, I feel a sense of accomplishment.

In my early teens, tying flies became a way of life. I found myself hunched over at the vise almost every day—sometimes for several hours at a sitting. I eventually ended up with so many flies that I decided to sell them to friends and family to scrape up enough money to buy more materials to support my habit.

In 1982, I purchased Jack Dennis' *Western Trout Fly Tying Manual, Volume 2* in an effort to further my education and become a more proficient and well-rounded tier. I lived vicariously through him by reading his books. In the early 1990s, I met Jack Dennis at the Complete Angler, in Englewood, Colorado, where he was conducting a fly tying and casting demonstration. Attending his seminar further solidified that I wanted to make a career out of fly fishing. My ambition was to become like Jack Dennis—tie flies commercially, guide, conduct seminars throughout the country, and write.

After I stockpiled hundreds of flies, I began to looking for retail outlets to peddle them. This was a tough nut to crack, but

*My niche over the years has been designing and tying tailwater flies that fool hard-fished, selective trout. Most of my flies are easy to tie but they have been rigorously tested in Cheesman Canyon by some of the most discriminative trout in the world.* JAY NICHOLS

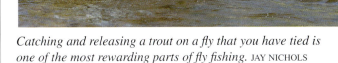

*Catching and releasing a trout on a fly that you have tied is one of the most rewarding parts of fly fishing.* JAY NICHOLS

Ken Walters, Bill Schappel, Terry and Lori Nicholson, Jackson Streit, and Bill Grems were all kind enough to buy my flies. From there, I began filling regular orders for several fly shops in the Denver metropolitan area.

Twenty years ago, the next phase of my fly-fishing career began as I started guiding customers out of the Blue Quill Angler fly shop in Evergreen, Colorado. Becoming a fly-fishing guide was a lifelong dream of mine. When I began, I was the last man in the guide rotation, picking up the crumbs behind veteran guides like Kevin Gregory, Monroe Coleman, and Randy Smith, and those early days were lean. After three seasons, I was able to spend four to five days on the river guiding customers and tying flies to generate some additional income to help support my family, though during those early years, my wife was the breadwinner. Without her blood, sweat, and tears, my guiding and fly-tying career would have been long gone.

My biggest breakthrough was when Ed Rolka decided to retire from commercially tying the Breadcrust Nymph and allowed me to carry on his tradition of tying the pattern. Very few tiers attempt to tie this pattern, let alone commercially, because red-phase ruffed grouse is hard to come by and the preparation of the quill is dangerous and tedious. As the old saying goes—you must be careful what you wish for. I went from wanting to sell a few flies to being overwhelmed with orders. Like many other commercial fly tiers I know, I bit off more than I could chew. At one point, during the peak of my commercial fly-tying career, I was producing about 28,000 flies each year, with about 25 percent of those flies being Breadcrust Nymphs. To fill my orders, I was burning the midnight oil and tying flies before and after guided trips or whenever I had spare time.

Looking back, I feel blessed to have spent so much time on the water guiding clients and tying thousands of dozens of flies. I still spend about 200 days a year on the water guiding clients, hosting destination trips, and enjoying personal days with my friends. I still tie a few custom fly orders and still tie flies commercially, but on a much smaller scale.

In writing this book, I would like to provide readers with step-by-step tutorials for tying some of the proven "guide flies" that I have used for the past 20 years. Many of these flies are my own innovations that surfaced from trying to solve the day-to-day problems that I have encountered on trout streams while guiding clients. My patterns are simple, and many of them would not win a fly-tying contest if judged on technical proficiency and difficulty. But they catch trout, which is the common goal of all good trout flies. Because I would rather spend time on the water than time at my fly-tying bench, most of the patterns use only a handful of materials and take only a few steps to tie.

While simplicity has always been a trademark of mine, I also like to incorporate some flash into my fly design. I frequently use glass or metal beads, Krystal Flash, Pearl Braid, Flashabou, Mylar tinsel, Glamour Madera, and other flashy materials. I feel that a dash of flash imitates characteristics of the emerging aquatic insects and helps the flies attract and fool hard-fished, selective trout.

Over my many years of commercial fly tying, I have developed some tying techniques and tricks (and certainly borrowed many from fellow professionals) that I share in this book. Hopefully these strategies will simplify things, save you time, and make the tying process more enjoyable. Fly tying is really only as difficult as you make it. My goal is to provide you with the proper tools and techniques to tie the best flies possible. After you familiarize yourself with these concepts you'll need to practice them to become proficient. With that in mind, strive for per-

*Fred Miller landed this huge Taylor River rainbow on a tiny midge larva. When there is a shortfall of* Mysis *shrimp flowing from the base of the dam, trout supplement their diet with tiny midges and mayflies. This is a tailwater angler's dream.*

fection on all your flies. Putting a mediocre fly into your fly box is not the way to become a better fly tier. If any of your flies are not properly proportioned, fix the problem immediately or cut the materials off the hook with a razor blade and start over.

Though many of the patterns in this book are of my own design, some of them are designed by others. But they have become personal favorites because they are so successful on the streams that I fish. Patterns such as the RS2, Buckskin, Griffith's Gnat, Breadcrust, Nuclear Egg, and many others are critical for success 365 days a year, and I would not be able to guide without them.

And, just to shake things up, I've also included a chapter containing two of my favorite attractors—the Limeade and Renegade. While fishing small flies has traditionally been my bread and butter, many of the rivers that I fish and guide on require a good attractor. The Limeade is a hair-wing pattern of my own design, tied specifically for high floatation and visibility. Simplicity, ease of tying, and effectiveness make the Renegade another life-long favorite. Late-summer success often requires pounding fish up or fishing dry-and-dropper rigs in skinny water where traditional nymphing rigs are not effective, and the Renegade is an excellent indicator pattern.

Another important aspect of this book is my thoughts on how to choose the appropriate fly based on the prevailing conditions. Whether you are imitating a midge pupa, an emerging *Baetis,* or mayfly adult, having the right fly at the right time can make or break your trip. Having fished the South Platte for most of my life, I've been challenged to fool some of the most selective trout in the West. From my past experiences, there has been little room for error. South Platte trout are finicky, super-selective, and difficult to fool. If you can catch trout on the South Platte, you can catch fish anywhere in the world.

In addition to sharing how I choose my patterns on the water, I also cover how to rig them under a wide range of conditions to ensure success. In the following pages, I provide a detailed orientation into nymphing rigs and how to fish them. I also elaborate on dry-and-dropper rigs and dry-fly and nymphing strategies. My objective is to introduce you to all the nitty-gritty information that will maximize your results on the stream, which includes leader and tippet selection, knots, spacing between your flies, and terminal tackle options such as weight and strike indicators. Knowing when, why, and how to fish these rigs, and making the appropriate adjustments, is an important aspect of telling the story of these fly patterns.

This book is not a beginning fly-tying manual. While many of my patterns are simple—just thread, wire, and dubbed fur—and easy to tie, patterns like Amy's Ant, Bead-Head Breadcrust Nymph, and Paper Tiger Stonefly will most likely challenge you. They are not difficult by any stretch of the imagination—but they do require several steps, some patience, manual dexterity, proper execution of materials, and some good hand-eye coordination.

If you want to learn the fundamentals of fly tying, I highly recommend taking a fly-tying class and purchasing a copy of *Charlie Craven's Basic Fly Tying*. Craven's book is in a league of its own and provides a solid orientation into a wide range of techniques for all abilities, enabling you to produce an assortment of flies that catch fish under a wide range of circumstances.

To become a proficient fly tier or accomplished angler takes serious commitment. There is no shortcut to success. Tying flies is not hard, but it takes repetition to master. You'll need to tie dozens of a single pattern before you reach a sense of accomplishment.

I recommend tying your flies by the half-dozen or dozen. This is important for two reasons: First, tying several flies at one time develops continuity, allowing you to tweak your flies and make minor adjustments. Your flies will get better after you get into a rhythm and become accustomed to working with the materials. If you are tying different sizes of the same fly, tie the larger sizes first. This makes the tying process much easier than diving right in and tying a size 22. Second, tying six or twelve flies almost guarantees that you will not run out of a "hot" fly on the river. Keep a stock some of your favorites—it's much easier to pull them from plastic bins instead of trying to fill holes in your fly box during the height of the season. There is nothing more frustrating than running out of the right fly at the wrong time.

Thank you for the opportunity to share some of my favorite flies with you. I hope that these step-by-step tutorials coupled with the tying and fishing tips will improve your tying and fishing skills. In many cases, having the right fly is only half the equation for success. Knowing how and when to fish it is equally important. Hopefully a few of these patterns will end up in your fly box and you'll have as much confidence in them as I do.

Pat Dorsey
Parker, Colorado 2010

# CHAPTER 1

# Mercury Black Beauty

I developed the original Black Beauty in the early 1990s to imitate the heavy concentrations of midge pupae found below deep, bottom-release reservoirs such as the South Platte below Cheesman Dam (Deckers), the Blue below Dillon Dam, and the San Juan below Navajo Dam. In its embryonic form, the Black Beauty had no name; it was just a black midge pupa pattern that had earned a spot in my fly box because it was easy to tie, durable, and, most importantly, it consistently fooled hard-fished trout.

In March 1992, Bob Saile, Scott Ratcliff, and I named my generic fly the Black Beauty after a trip on the Blue River near Silverthorne, Colorado. On that trip we caught numerous *Mysis*-fed trout between 16 and 20 inches, but one trout in par-ticular really stood out. Saile hooked and landed an 8-pound rainbow on my small black midge in a deep slot right below the I-70 bridge. Saile's rainbow looked like a slab of bacon—it was 26 inches long and had an 18-inch girth. To date, it is one of the most impressive rainbows I've ever seen caught on the Blue River near Silverthorne.

As we were driving home on the mountain roads and rem-iniscing about our great day, Ratliff said, "We really caught some beauties today. You ought to call your little black midge pupa the Black Beauty." The name stuck, and the Black Beauty has since become one of my favorite midge patterns.

Midges are one of the most important foods to imitate for tailwater anglers, because they are available to trout in huge

The Black Beauty imitates a midge pupa. You can create variations to match the midges in your local stream by simply changing colors of materials, or even beads. Clockwise from left to right: brown, black, and pale-olive Black Beauties, Mercury Black Beauty, Flashback Mercury Black Beauty, and Bead-Head Black Beauty (recipes at the end of the chapter). JAY NICHOLS

*Terry Escamilla fooled this beautiful rainbow on the North Fork of the South Platte River with a Mercury Black Beauty. A #16 orange Nuclear Egg dropped with a #22 Mercury Black Beauty is one of my favorite rigs for this watershed.*

*The Black Beauty is one of my go-to flies for tailwaters. Anglers will find huge concentrations of midge pupae for several miles below deep, bottom-release tailwaters like Cheesman Dam.*

numbers on a year-round basis. In North America, there are an estimated 3,500 species of aquatic Diptera, which outnumber mayflies, caddisflies, and stoneflies combined. Three families are important to anglers: Chironomidae (midges), Tipulidae (crane flies), and Simuliidae (black flies). The Black Beauty is an effective imitation for midge pupae and black-fly larvae. The dubbed thorax area imitates the swollen wings and legs of the emerging adult. Midge pupae are shorter and more robust than the wormlike larvae. Their abdomens are segmented with highly visible wing pads that slant downward.

Many anglers underestimate midges as an important food source because of their size, but what midges lack in size, they make up in numbers. Not only do millions of midges pupate on a daily basis, but they also fill an important void when other aquatic insects and terrestrials are unavailable to trout. When midges are emerging, trout suspend in the upper third of the water column and eat a countless number of pupae with minimal effort. In my experience, trout eat considerably more pupae than both larvae and adults, since it makes no sense for them to chase the occasional larva or expend energy rising toward

the surface to eat the sporadic adult when the pupae are so abundant. However, adult and larva patterns can be important at times.

Before emergence, midge pupae become fidgety, moving up and down in the water column. They repeat this restless behavior several times before they make their final ascent to emerge into adults. When the pupae prepare for emergence, they hang down in a C shape with their thoraxes pressed against the meniscus until they break free from their pupal sheaths and become adults.

While the original Black Beauty imitates a midge pupa remarkably well, the addition of a clear, silver-lined glass bead provides an even more realistic imitation of the emerging pupa. As the emerging pupa makes its way toward the surface, highly reflective air is trapped beneath the outer layer of nymphal skin, especially toward the thorax. This mirrorlike bubble, imitated by the bead, helps the emerging midge propel itself toward the meniscus.

Adding a piece of pearl Flashabou to the top of the Mercury Black Beauty increases the effectiveness of this pattern by magnifying the natural translucency of an emerging midge's abdomen. The extra flash seems to account for more strikes, and it has become my favorite in the Black Beauty series. I frequently use the Flashback Mercury Black Beauty during non-hatch periods too, and it is an excellent attractor in a two-fly nymphing rig. The Flashback Mercury Black Beauty has saved the day on many Western tailwaters when the water was slightly off-color from spring runoff, fluctuating flows as a result of downstream irrigation demand, or in the aftermath of an afternoon rain shower.

The Zebra Midge, invented by Ted Welling, is a close cousin of the Black Beauty, and I often use it when I need a pupa that sinks quickly. In faster currents, especially when fishing dry-and-dropper rigs, I frequently use the Zebra Midge as an attractor when nothing is hatching or when midges are hatching sporadically, because it has a quicker sink rate than flies with glass beads. The Zebra Midge may also be dropped off an attractor like a San Juan Worm, egg, scud, crane fly, or stonefly to draw some additional attention to it. The trout are drawn in by the attractor, but typically eat the smaller fly (at least in midge-ridden waters).

One particularly effective technique when you see fish feeding on both adult midges and pupae below the surface is to drop a Zebra Midge off a #18-20 heavily hackled Griffith's Gnat or other midge cluster pattern. In skinny water, a traditional two-fly nymphing rig tends to spook trout, whereas the dry-and-dropper rig generally does not. Once the trout have started to consistently eat midge adults, cut off the Zebra Midge and fish only the Griffith's Gnat.

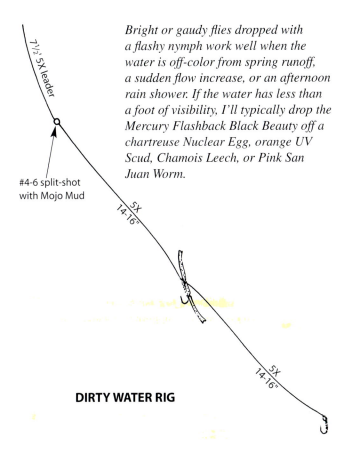

*Bright or gaudy flies dropped with a flashy nymph work well when the water is off-color from spring runoff, a sudden flow increase, or an afternoon rain shower. If the water has less than a foot of visibility, I'll typically drop the Mercury Flashback Black Beauty off a chartreuse Nuclear Egg, orange UV Scud, Chamois Leech, or Pink San Juan Worm.*

**DIRTY WATER RIG**

## RIGGING AND FISHING TIPS

The Black Beauty (and its variations) fish well under a wide range of conditions, regardless of the season. It is especially effective at the beginning of a midge hatch. Once you begin to see adults, you should switch from a larva to a pupa pattern

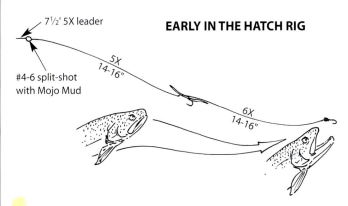

**EARLY IN THE HATCH RIG**

*In the initial phases of a midge hatch, I typically drop my Mercury Black Beauty off a larger attractor such as a UV Scud, Nuclear Egg, or San Juan Worm to draw attention to the smaller fly. I use a size 4 or 6 split-shot.*

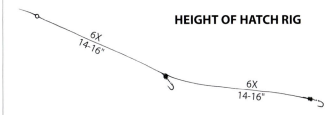

**HEIGHT OF HATCH RIG**

*As the hatch intensifies, I drop the Black Beauty off another midge larva or pupa anticipating that the trout are feeding selectively on midges. I'll typically fish my pupa in the point-fly position, which is farther from the weight, because they naturally drift higher in the water column.*

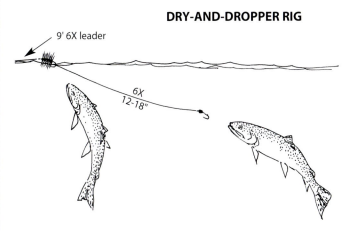

**DRY-AND-DROPPER RIG**

*One of my favorite dry-and-dropper combinations is a heavily hackled Griffith's Gnat dropped with a midge pupa like a Mercury Flashback Black Beauty, Bead-Head Black Beauty (tungsten bead), or Zebra Midge.*

*I carry several color variations of the Mercury Black Beauty in my fly boxes. The most effective colors include brown, pale olive, olive, gray, and black.* JAY NICHOLS

like a Black Beauty. As the hatch intensifies, you'll generally catch more fish by drifting your pupa through the top third of the water column, but early on fish it closer to the bottom.

Under normal conditions, I typically concentrate my efforts in the transitional zones—mid-channel shelves and gravel bars—that funnel into deeper slots and pools. The most aggressive midge feeders are typically positioned on the drop-off, which is easily identified by the color change. It is not uncommon to see two different sizes of midges (#18 and #22) hatching during the spring, and you may need to fish two different sizes of pupa to match the hatch. I refer to the larger variety common in Colorado as the big spring midge. This midge is so large many anglers confuse the adult for a Blue-Winged Olive. From my past experiences, trout tend to key on the larger variety during the spring. But conditions change depending on the drainage. As the larger spring midges run their course, trout key on the smaller midges for the rest of the season. If you have any doubt as to which size of midge the trout are keying on, use a stomach pump to remove any uncertainty.

When fish are keying on pupae, they're typically feeding midcolumn as opposed to feeding near the bottom of the substrate. Adjusting your weight is critical. Too much or too little weight can make or break your success. It is not uncommon for anglers to fish too much weight and drift their flies below the trout's feeding zone.

Dry-and-dropper rigs are another effective way to suspend a midge pupa and are especially effective when flows are low and clear or trout have become sensitive or suspicious of conventional strike-indicator rigs. They also allow anglers to fish skinny water where they would not traditionally be able to fish standard nymphing rigs.

This is the perfect scenario for a Bead-Head Black Beauty tied with a tungsten bead. I'll typically suspend the pupa on 18 to 24 inches of 6X tippet off the bend of a large dry fly such as an Elk-Hair Caddis, Stimulator, or Amy's Ant, or a heavily hackled #18 Griffith's Gnat during a midge hatch.

Whether you use a strike indicator or a dry fly, most of your strikes will go undetected if you rely strictly on your strike indicator to determine whether a trout has taken your fly. This is especially true in slower currents, where it takes considerably longer for the slack between the flies and the strike indicator to tighten. Successful anglers look for flashes or any movement, opening mouths, or lifts in the water column that indicate a potential take.

### Mercury Black Beauty

| | |
|---|---|
| Hook: | #18-24 Tiemco 101 |
| Bead: | Clear, silver-lined glass bead (extra small) |
| Thread: | Black 8/0 Uni-Thread |
| Abdomen: | Black 8/0 Uni-Thread |
| Rib: | Fine (#18-20) or extra fine (#22-24) Lagartun copper wire |
| Thorax: | Black Superfine |

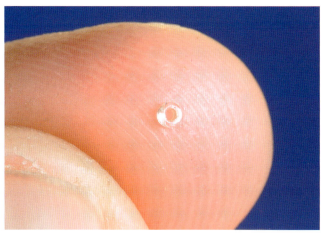

**1.** Place a few beads on your fly-tying table with the openings up. Press your index finger firmly on top of a bead so that it sticks to your finger.

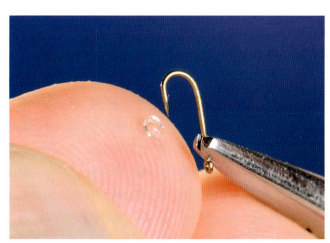

**2.** To make it easier to handle the small hook, clamp a pair of forceps onto the hook near the eye. Tilt the hook upright (with the hook bend up) and put the hook point into the opening of the bead. With your finger, slide the bead around the hook bend toward the eye.

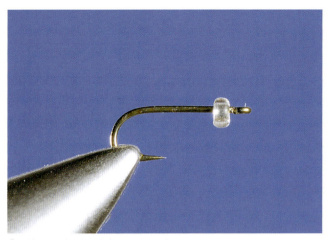

**3.** Clamp the hook into your vise.

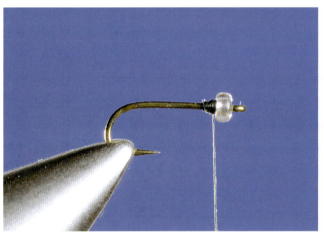

**4.** Attach the thread behind the bead. Build a slight taper between the hook shank and the bead to hold it in place.

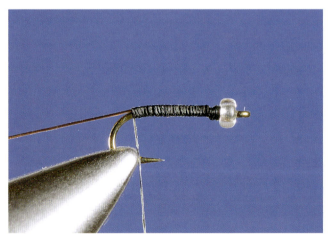

**5.** Tie in a 6-inch piece of copper wire on top of the hook shank behind the bead. Wrap the thread back in tight, symmetrical turns over the copper wire, keeping the wire on top of the hook shank. Aim for a smooth abdomen.

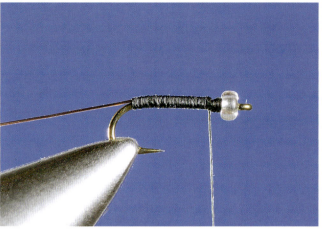

**6.** Wrap the thread forward, making sure there is no exposed copper wire. Wraps should be tight and equally proportioned.

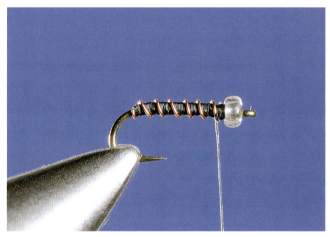

**7.** Wrap the wire forward (reverse rib) six or seven times. Secure the copper wire behind the glass bead with four tight wraps of thread. Clip the excess wire and bury the butt end.

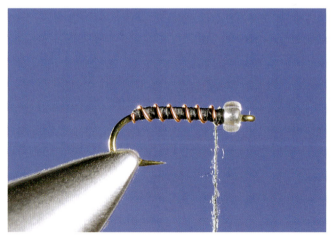

**8.** Twist a thin and sparse dubbing noodle.

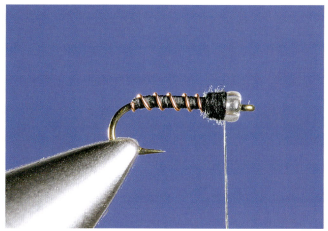

**9.** Dub a slightly tapered thorax between the abdomen and bead. Take four tight wraps with the thread to produce a clean collar behind the bead. Whip-finish and clip the thread.

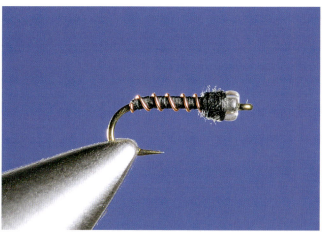

**10.** The thread abdomen should be smooth and uniform from the hook bend to the thorax with six or seven evenly spaced turns of copper wire. The tightly dubbed thorax should be equal to the diameter of the bead.

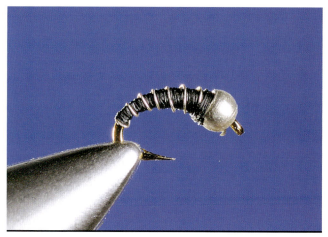

### *Zebra Midge*

| | |
|---|---|
| Hook: | #18-24 Tiemco 2487 |
| Thread: | Black 8/0 Uni-Thread |
| Abdomen: | Black 8/0 Uni-Thread |
| Rib: | Fine (#18-20) or extra fine (#22-24) Lagartun silver wire |

Note: To date, the Zebra Midge is one of the most popular midge patterns at Lee's Ferry, especially dropped off an orange scud, San Juan Worm, or egg pattern. Since you can tie it easily after learning the Mercury Black Beauty, I include it here. The Zebra Midge has become a favorite from coast to coast on tailwaters, spring creeks, and freestone streams.

### *Flashback Mercury Black Beauty (Gray)*

| | |
|---|---|
| Hook: | #18-24 Tiemco 2488 |
| Bead: | Clear, silver-lined glass bead (extra small) |
| Thread: | Gray 8/0 Uni-Thread |
| Abdomen: | Gray 8/0 Uni-Thread |
| Flashback: | Pearl Mylar |
| Rib: | Fine (#18-20) or extra fine (#22-24) Lagartun copper wire |
| Thorax: | Gray Superfine |

## Mercury Black Beauty

| | |
|---|---|
| Hook: | #18-24 Tiemco 101 |
| Thread: | Black 8/0 Uni-Thread |
| Abdomen: | Black 8/0 Uni-Thread |
| Rib: | Fine (#18-20) or extra fine (#22-24) Lagartun copper wire |
| Thorax: | Black Superfine |

Note: Pictured in the group shot on page 1.

## Bead-Head Black Beauty

| | |
|---|---|
| Hook: | #18-24 Tiemco 2488 |
| Bead: | Black tungsten bead (1.5 and 2mm) or black glass bead |
| Thread: | Black 8/0 Uni-Thread |
| Abdomen: | Black 8/0 Uni-Thread |
| Rib: | Fine (#18-20) or extra fine (#22-24) Lagartun copper wire |
| Thorax: | Black Superfine |

Note: Pictured in the group shot on page 1.

## Black Beauty (Brown)

| | |
|---|---|
| Hook: | #18-24 Tiemco 101 |
| Thread: | Brown 8/0 Uni-Thread |
| Abdomen: | Brown 8/0 Uni-Thread |
| Rib: | Fine (#18-20) or extra fine (#22-24) Lagartun copper wire |
| Thorax: | Brown Superfine |

Note: Pictured in the group shot on page 1.

## Black Beauty (Pale-Olive)

| | |
|---|---|
| Hook: | #18-24 Tiemco 101 |
| Thread: | Light-cahill 8/0 Uni-Thread |
| Abdomen: | Light-cahill 8/0 Uni-Thread |
| Rib: | Fine (#18-20) or extra fine (#22-24) Lagartun copper wire |
| Thorax: | Olive Superfine |

Note: Pictured in the group shot on page 1.

## Flashback Mercury Black Beauty

| | |
|---|---|
| Hook: | #18-24 Tiemco 101 |
| Bead: | Clear, silver-lined glass bead (extra small) |
| Thread: | Black 8/0 Uni-Thread |
| Abdomen: | Black 8/0 Uni-Thread |
| Flashback: | Pearl Mylar |
| Rib: | Fine (#18-20) or extra fine (#22-24) Lagartun copper wire |
| Thorax: | Black Superfine |

Note: Pictured in the group shot on page 1.

## Mercury Zebra Midge

| | |
|---|---|
| Hook: | #18-24 Tiemco 2487 |
| Bead: | Clear, silver-lined glass bead (extra small) |
| Thread: | Black 8/0 Uni-Thread |
| Abdomen: | Black 8/0 Uni-Thread |
| Rib: | Fine (#18-20) or extra fine (#22-24) Lagartun silver wire |
| Thorax: | Black Superfine |

# CHAPTER 2

# Mercury Midge

Back in the mid-1990s, Bill Black, president of Spirit River, sent me a plastic bag filled with an assortment of small glass beads. There were several colors and sizes—all applicable for tying tiny mayfly and midge imitations. "Nobody has these yet," said Black. "Experiment with them, and let me know what you think."

One glass bead in particular—the clear, silver-lined one—caught my attention. Wheels began to turn, and I immediately headed to my fly-tying room. I put an extra-small one on a #20 scud hook and proceeded to tie a midge larva pattern similar to an old South Platte standby called the String Thing.

The String Thing is like the Miracle Nymph (another popular midge larva designed for the South Platte), with the excep-

tion of the prominent black head. The String Thing and Miracle Nymph are proven larva imitations made of only wire and thread, but both of them have been plucked from some of the most selective trout in the West.

When I looked at the completed fly, which was only a String Thing with a clear, silver-lined glass bead, the thorax resembled a tiny thermometer tube filled with mercury, and I quickly named my new little midge the Mercury Midge.

The following week, I took the Mercury Midge to the South Platte River in Cheesman Canyon and tested it rigorously. I was pleasantly surprised to see discriminating rainbows move 8 to 10 inches to intercept it. Immediately, I knew there was something special about the bead that persuaded trout to eat this fly,

*The Mercury Midge can be tied in a variety of colors to imitate both midge larvae and pupae, including pale olive, olive-brown, black, and original (recipes at the end of the chapter).* JAY NICHOLS

*I have fooled countless trout with Mercury Midges in size 20 and 22. Don't let the simplicity of the pattern fool you—it's deadly in pressured waters.* JAY NICHOLS

*Hi-Lite glass beads are distributed by Spirit River. The Quick Silver SL (silver-lined) bead closely resembles a glass tube filled with mercury, after which the Mercury series was named. Many fly tiers, including myself, refer to Hi-Lite Quick Silver bead as the "mercury bead." Diamond Killer Caddis Beads are similar.*

# TANDEM RIGS

Although anglers have been experimenting with multiple-fly rigs for centuries, they did not become popular until the mid-1980s. Now, tandem rigs are accepted as the norm; in fact, it's rare to find an angler not fishing a two-fly nymphing rig.

For my upper fly, I typically fish with an attractor that draws attention to the lower fly, which imitates what the trout are accustomed to seeing and eating on a regular basis. I typically choose my attractor based on the prevailing hatch. For instance, if caddis are hatching, I'll use a caddis larva or pupa, or if Yellow Sallies are migrating toward the river's edge to transform into adults, I'll choose a Yellow Sally nymph. If scuds and aquatic worms are getting dislodged from erratic flows, I'll use a scud or San Juan Worm. When there is no apparent hatch, I'll often fish with a flashy mayfly nymph or midge as my attractor.

In a two-fly rig, I believe you get a better hook-up when you connect them eye to eye, especially on #22-26 nymphs. This method reduces the possibility of any monofilament or fluorocarbon tippet getting in the way of a good hook-up, because the hook gap and point are free of any obstructions.

My second fly is generally a small, #18-22 mayfly or midge pattern that imitates what is most abundant at the given time. If there is a good Blue-Winged Olive hatch, and *Baetis* nymphs are emerging, I'll fish a Sparkle Wing RS2 or Barr Emerger. If there is a strong midge hatch, I'll use a midge pupa for my dropper fly. I typically keep my flies spaced between 14 and 16 inches apart.

Most of the time, I fish with a two-fly rig, but when conditions are tough, such as slow fishing or off-color water, I fish three flies because the third fly increases my odds of catching more trout. I also attach a third fly, from time to time, to test some of my new patterns without compromising my success.

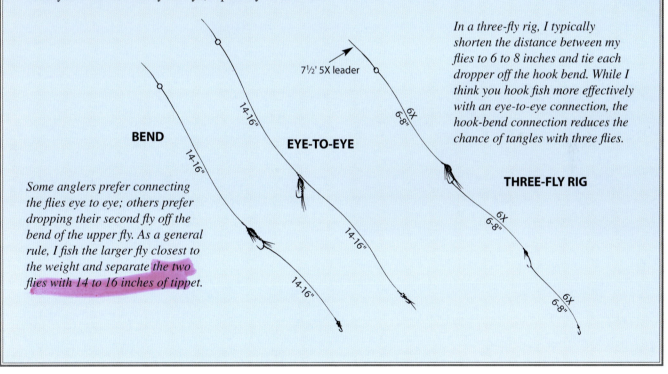

**BEND**

*Some anglers prefer connecting the flies eye to eye; others prefer dropping their second fly off the bend of the upper fly. As a general rule, I fish the larger fly closest to the weight and separate the two flies with 14 to 16 inches of tippet.*

**EYE-TO-EYE**

7½' 5X leader

14-16"

14-16"

14-16"

14-16"

6X
6-8"

6X
6-8"

6X
6-8"

*In a three-fly rig, I typically shorten the distance between my flies to 6 to 8 inches and tie each dropper off the hook bend. While I think you hook fish more effectively with an eye-to-eye connection, the hook-bend connection reduces the chance of tangles with three flies.*

**THREE-FLY RIG**

but I could not put my finger on it. Later it occurred to me that the silver-lined glass bead imitated the gas bubble that gets trapped in the midge's thorax when it emerges.

According to J. R. Harris, in *An Angler's Entomology* (1956), "The end of the hatching nymph . . . assumes a much increased luster, and in fact it strongly resembles a section of glass tube which has been filled with mercury. This effect is even more noticeable in pupae and those long-legged midges, the chironomids." Interestingly, I noticed the similarity to mercury just as J. R. Harris did.

Ralph Cutter's DVD, *Bugs of the Underworld,* demonstrates this phenomenon well. His footage shows an emerging midge becoming fidgety and restless, moving up and down in the water column, and the noticeable gas bubble that forms before the pupa emerges into an adult. The mercury beads on the Mercury Midge and Mercury Black Beauty imitate this gas bubble perfectly.

After discovering the success of the Mercury Midge, I put clear, silver-lined glass beads on other patterns like RS2s, Pheasant Tails, Brassies, Buckskins, cased caddisflies, blood

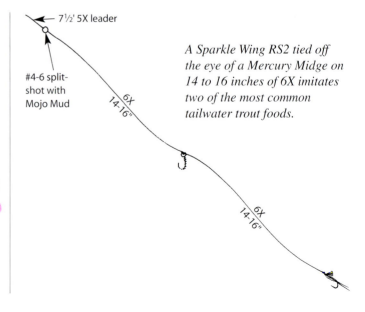

*Dr. Mark Adams fishes with one of my favorite rigs in Cheesman Canyon: a Mercury Midge dropped with a Sparkle Wing RS2. This rig is especially effective in slower tailouts and pools where the trout have longer to inspect your artificials.*

*John Keefover fooled this Arkansas rainbow with a Mercury Midge several miles below Pueblo Reservoir. Mercury Midges fish well year-round, but they are especially effective from November through March.*

midges, *Baetis* nymphs, and Pale Morning Dun nymphs. Umpqua Feather Merchants picked up the entire line and called it the Mercury Series. These patterns, like the original Mercury Midge, have also proven to catch a lot of trout.

### RIGGING AND FISHING TIPS

I typically fish the Mercury Midge as an attractor in a two-fly nymphing rig, frequently with a mayfly emerger such as a Sparkle Wing RS2 so that I can imitate the two most important food groups found on trout streams: midges and mayflies. Early in the day I dredge my flies in the deeper slots and hearts of the runs, and as the hatches intensify, I move toward the riffles and mid-channel shelves and gravel bars and fish less weight.

If the trout are keying on larvae, I'll typically fish with either the white or pale-olive Mercury Midge. As the hatch intensifies, the olive-brown and black Mercury Midges seem to fish better as the trout begin to intercept more pupae.

7½' 5X leader

#4-6 split-shot with Mojo Mud

6X
14-16"

6X
14-16"

*A Sparkle Wing RS2 tied off the eye of a Mercury Midge on 14 to 16 inches of 6X imitates two of the most common tailwater trout foods.*

## Mercury Midge

Hook:            #18-22 Tiemco 2487
Bead:            Clear, silver-lined glass bead (extra small)
Thread:          White 6/0 Flymaster Plus
Abdomen:         White 6/0 Flymaster Plus
Rib:             Fine (#18-20) or extra fine (#22-24)
                 Lagartun copper wire

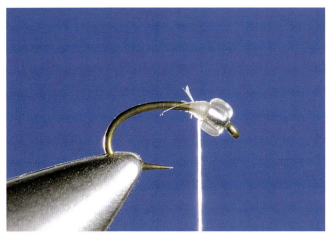

**1.** After placing the bead on the hook, clamp the hook into your vise and slide the bead toward the hook eye. Attach the thread behind the bead and secure the bead with several wraps of thread.

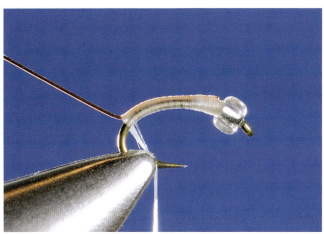

**2.** Attach the copper wire on top of the hook shank and wrap the thread back over the wire toward the hook bend. Keep the wire on the top of the hook shank and make your wraps tight and symmetrical to form a smooth abdomen.

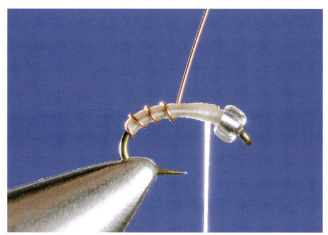

**3.** Wrap the thread forward and leave it behind the bead. Make sure no exposed copper wire shows through the thread. Begin wrapping the wire forward, aiming for symmetrical turns.

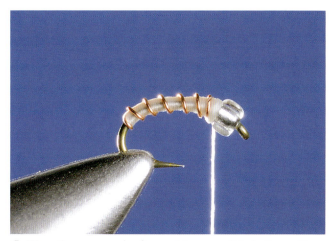

**4.** Wrap the copper wire forward (reverse rib) six times. Keep the ribbing spaced evenly throughout the abdomen. Tie off and clip the wire, burying the butt end. Smooth out the taper between the abdomen and the bead with thread.

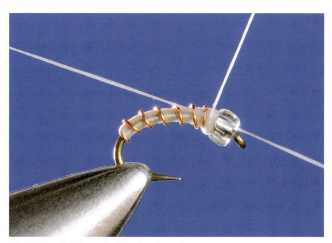

**5.** Whip-finish and clip the thread.

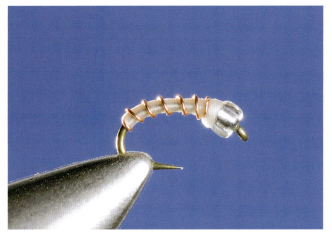

**6.** The Mercury Midge's abdomen should be uniform throughout with seven or eight evenly spaced wraps of copper wire. As you whip-finish the fly, develop a small taper between the abdomen and the bead.

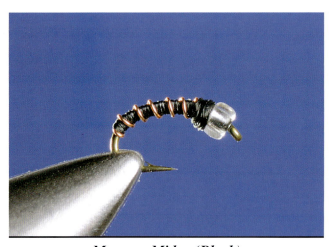

### Mercury Midge (Black)

Hook:       #18-#22 Tiemco 2487
Bead:       Clear, silver-lined glass bead (extra small)
Thread:     Black 8/0 Uni-Thread
Abdomen:    Black 8/0 Uni-Thread
Rib:        Fine (#18-20) or extra fine (#22-24)
            Lagartun copper wire

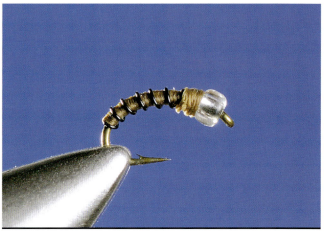

### Mercury Midge (Olive-Brown)

Hook:       #18-22 Tiemco 2487
Bead:       Clear, silver-lined glass bead (extra small)
Thread:     Olive-brown (#60) 6/0 Danville
Abdomen:    Olive-brown (#60) 6/0 Danville
Rib:        Small (#18-20) or extra small (#22-24)
            black Uni Wire

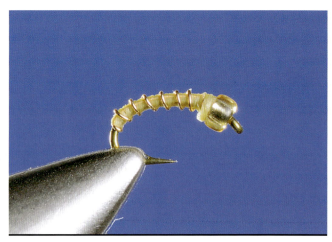

### Mercury Midge (Pale Olive)

Hook:       #18-22 Tiemco 2487
Bead:       Gold, silver-lined glass bead (extra small)
Thread:     Light-cahill 8/0 Uni-Thread
Abdomen:    Light-cahill 8/0 Uni-Thread
Rib:        Fine (#18-20) or extra fine (#22-24)
            Lagartun copper wire

# CHAPTER 3

# Mercury Blood Midge

If you fish tailwaters on a regular basis, you'll need a good bloodworm or blood midge imitation. I have enjoyed a lot of success with this pattern from the San Juan in northern New Mexico to the Bighorn in southern Montana. It's the ultimate guide fly—easy to tie, durable, and fools trout with regularity.

Midge larvae are found in a wide range of colors—red, pale-olive, gray, brown, cream, brown, and black. According to Leonard C. Ferrington Jr., a professor at the Department of Entomology at the University of Minnesota, "Midge larval densities depend on month of year, productivity of stream, and kinds of stream-bottom substrates. Typical densities, however, may range from 800 to 2,000 larvae per square meter."

Unlike a midge pupa with its pronounced thorax, a larva has a uniform, segmented abdomen, which makes it look like a small worm. Larvae living in areas of a stream or lake with lower oxygen levels are commonly called bloodworms or blood midges because they contain hemoglobin and are bright red in color. Hemoglobin is the same oxygen-carrying pigment that makes our blood red. It allows members of the Chironomidae to store oxygen within their body to live in environments with little or no oxygen.

When analyzing the stomach contents of trout that I have caught on the Bighorn or San Juan River, there are generally several blood midges in each sample. Larvae occasionally drift, intentionally (for the purposes of redistribution) or uninten-

*This magnificent rainbow took a Mercury Blood Midge during the last week of March. The Mercury Blood Midge is one of my favorite winter flies.*

*I keep my fly boxes well-stocked with #18-22 Mercury Blood Midges.* JAY NICHOLS

# WEIGHT MATTERS

When I set up my nymphing rig, I start with a 7½- to 9-foot leader and add 14 to 16 inches of tippet with a blood or surgeon's knot. I leave the tag ends about ⅛-inch long and put a #4 or #6 split-shot above the knot, which keeps it from sliding down my leader toward my upper fly. When fishing for selective trout in clear water, I usually use fluorocarbon. I frequently adjust my weight with tungsten putty, such as John Perizzolo's Mojo Mud, molded around or above the split-shot to prevent it from moving on the leader. Avoid putting it on the leader in a cigar shape; otherwise, your tippet will spin in the water. I keep a chunk handy on my lanyard or my vest, which makes it easy to take off or add small pieces for slight adjustments in depth.

Many anglers think moldable putty is hard to work with and prefer split-shot as a more accurate method of weighting their rigs. In my opinion, putty alternatives are very easy to use. Whenever you are nymphing, you need to be in the right feeding zone to catch fish. More times than not, this requires fishing your flies near the bottom. As you do with split-shot, you add enough putty so that your flies occasionally tap the bottom. You should bounce on the bottom occasionally, but not get hung up. If you snag on the bottom, take some putty off. As the insects move higher in the water column, you may need to remove all the putty.

The advantage to putty is that you can fine-tune your weight quicker and more accurately than you can with split-shot. For instance, if you are fishing with three #4 split-shot and you take one shot off, you have made a 33 percent reduction in weight. With putty you can make smaller adjustments (5 to 10 percent) to ensure your flies are in the correct feeding zone. Plus, Mojo Mud is tungsten, which sinks faster than lead and is more environmentally friendly.

---

tionally (such as when they are dislodged during a flow increase or erratic flows). They also become available to trout when they transform into pupae. Blood midges may mature in a few weeks to a few months, depending on the water's temperature and chemistry. Once the pupa matures, the blood midge dislodges from the sediments and twists, turns, and wiggles its way to the surface. The thorax area (puparium) is filled with gases that provide buoyancy and assist in the ascent to the surface. Once again, the mercury bead imitates the appearance of the chrome-colored gas-filled pupal sheath.

## RIGGING AND FISHING TIPS

On my local waters—South Platte, Blue, Yampa, Frying Pan, and Williams Fork, to name only a few—the Mercury Blood Midge is one of my go-to winter flies. While the density of blood midge larvae is mind-boggling in some areas, they do not produce selective feeding like you would commonly associate with other varieties of aquatic Diptera, *Baetis*, PMDs, caddis, and stoneflies. In most cases, trout eat them opportunistically. I have found the Mercury Blood Midge works especially well during the pre- and post-spawn season. I typically begin fishing this pattern mid to late October through to mid April. The Mercury Blood Midge is one of my go-to patterns to entice fish migrating upstream from Elevenmile Reservoir in the spring.

I have fooled countless pre-spawn trout with this pattern, which leads me to believe they are eating this fly because of the color. In many cases, they'll eat the Mercury Blood Midge over an egg pattern because hordes of anglers fish egg patterns

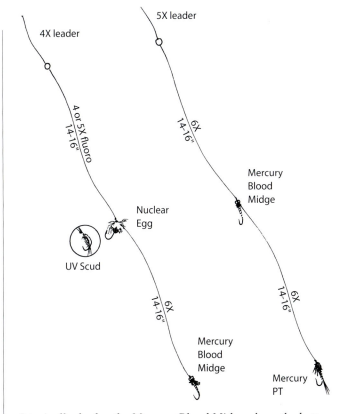

*I typically dredge the Mercury Blood Midge along the bottom where the highest number of blood midges dwell. When targeting pre- and post-spawning trout, I drop the Mercury Blood Midge off a UV Scud or Nuclear Egg.*

*The Mercury Blood Midge is one of my favorite flies on the Bighorn River below Yellowtail Dam. During the spring, I typically drop the Mercury Blood Midge off an orange scud.* KIM DORSEY

during the height of the spawning season and the trout become used to seeing too many of them. Early in the run, I typically drop the Mercury Blood Midge off an egg pattern, but during the peak of the spawning season, I'll drop a Mercury Pheasant Tail off the Mercury Blood Midge. This strategy has proven to be a deadly combination for lake-run fish.

Throughout the remaining part of the year, trout that are accustomed to eating blood midges rarely pass up the opportunity to eat one. They will eat blood midges any time of the day regardless of the conditions or the season. Under normal conditions (non-spawning periods or when the flows are within their normal historic levels and clear), I use the Mercury Blood Midge as a searching pattern or an attractor and drop a midge larva, pupa, or mayfly nymph off of it.

Other color variations such as black and olive work well, and chartreuse is especially effective when the green midges start hatching in mid June. This pattern is similar to the Green Machine that was invented by Bruce Stagg in the mid-1980s for the Spinney Mountain Ranch section of the South Platte to imitate the abundant lime-green midges that hatch in June and July. A #22-24 chartreuse Mercury Blood Midge fishes well in the mornings before Pale Morning Dun and Trico hatches.

## *Mercury Blood Midge*

| Hook: | #18-22 Tiemco 200R or #24 Dai-Riki 270 |
|---|---|
| Bead: | Clear, silver-lined glass bead (extra small) |
| Thread: | Red 8/0 Uni-Thread |
| Abdomen: | Red 8/0 Uni-Thread |
| Rib: | Fine (#18-20) or extra fine (#22-24) Lagartun gold wire |
| Thorax: | Peacock herl |
| Head: | Red 8/0 Uni-Thread colored with a black Sharpie |

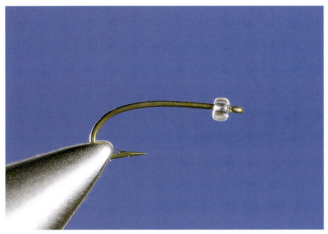

**1.** Put a glass bead on the hook and clamp it into your vise. Slide the bead toward the hook eye.

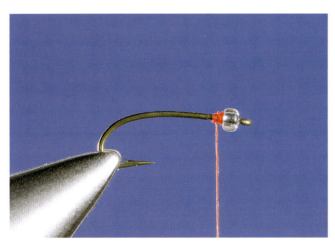

**2.** Attach your thread behind the bead and build a slight dam of thread behind the bead to hold it in place.

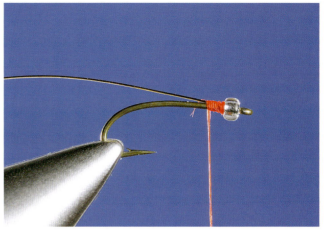

**3.** Tie a 6-inch piece of copper wire on top of the hook shank.

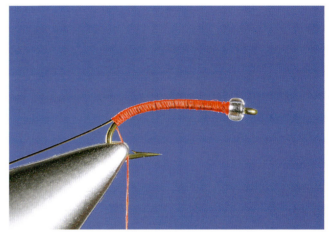

**4.** Wrap back over the copper wire toward the hook bend, keeping the wire on top of the hook shank. As you wrap the thread toward the hook bend, keep the wraps tight and symmetrical to form a smooth abdomen. Wrap the thread back one thread width at a time to ensure a smooth abdomen.

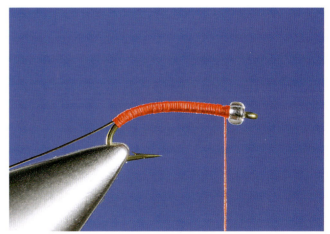

**5.** Wrap the thread forward and leave it behind the bead. Each consecutive wrap of thread should be in front of the last one. Make sure there is no exposed copper wire.

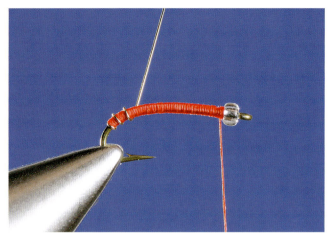

**6.** Wrap the copper wire forward (reverse rib) ten times. Keep the ribbing spaced evenly throughout the abdomen.

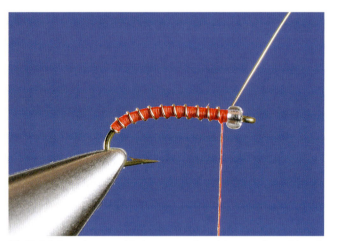

**7.** Hold the wire at a 45-degree angle with your thread hand. With your other hand, secure the wire with four tight wraps of thread.

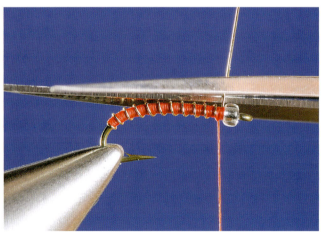

**8.** Clip the excess wire. If you use the back portion of your scissors, you will not dull the tips. With your index finger, pull the butt end of the wire back toward you so that it lies flat next to the bead. Bury the butt end with four wraps of thread.

**9.** Select a fluffy piece of peacock herl. The peacock collar should be approximately one hook gap wide.

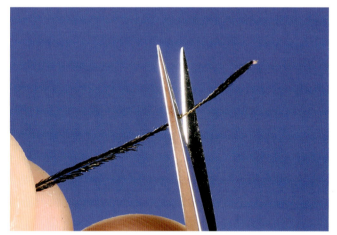

**10.** Pull off one piece of nice fluffy peacock herl and trim ½ inch off the tip.

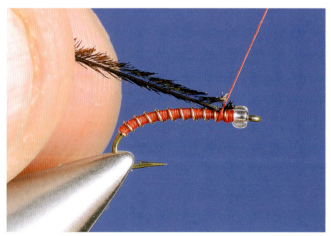

**11.** Hold the peacock herl with your index finger and thumb. Tie the peacock herl in tip first with four tight wraps of thread. The tip is more supple than the butt end of the peacock herl and produces a much better collar.

**12.** Wrap the peacock herl forward seven times. Each consecutive wrap should be in front of the preceding wrap to avoid matting down the herl.

**13.** Secure the peacock with four tight wraps of thread. Leave the thread hanging behind the bead.

**14.** Clip the butt end of the peacock herl. With four tight turns of thread, produce a smooth thread collar behind the bead. Pull the bobbin down, leaving 4 inches of thread dangling.

**15.** Hold the bobbin in your left hand to keep the thread taut. Using a Sharpie, color 2 inches of the thread black.

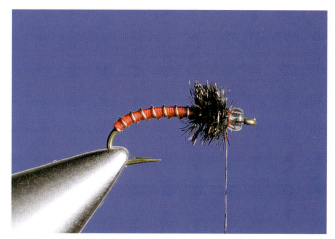

**16.** Let the thread dry for a few seconds before whip-finishing. Clip the excess thread.

**17.** The thread abdomen should be uniform and symmetrical from the hook bend to the thorax with eight or nine evenly spaced turns of copper wire exposed. The peacock collar should be full, finished with a smooth thread band between the collar and bead.

## *Mercury Blood Midge (Black)*

| | |
|---|---|
| Hook: | #18-22 Tiemco 200R or #24 Dai-Riki 270 |
| Bead: | Clear, silver-lined glass bead (extra small) |
| Thread: | Black 8/0 Uni-Thread |
| Abdomen: | Black 8/0 Uni-Thread |
| Rib: | Fine (#18-20) or extra fine (#22-24) Lagartun gold wire |
| Thorax: | Peacock herl |
| Head: | Black 8/0 Uni-Thread |

## *Mercury Blood Midge (Olive-Brown)*

| | |
|---|---|
| Hook: | #18-22 Tiemco 200R or #24 Dai-Riki 270 |
| Bead: | Clear, silver-lined glass bead (extra small) |
| Thread: | Olive-brown (#60) 6/0 Danville |
| Abdomen: | Olive-brown (#60) 6/0 Danville |
| Rib: | Fine (#18-20) or extra fine (#22-24) Lagartun gold wire |
| Thorax: | Peacock herl |
| Head: | Olive-brown (#60) 6/0 Danville colored with a black Sharpie |

## *Mercury Blood Midge (Olive)*

| | |
|---|---|
| Hook: | #18-22 Tiemco 200R or #24 Dai-Riki 270 |
| Bead: | Clear, silver-lined glass bead (extra small) |
| Thread: | Chartreuse 6/0 Danville |
| Abdomen: | Olive 8/0 Uni-Thread |
| Rib: | Fine (#18-20) or extra fine (#22-24) Lagartun gold wire |
| Thorax: | Peacock herl |
| Head: | Chartreuse 6/0 Danville colored with a black Sharpie |

# CHAPTER 4

# *Top Secret Midge*

The Top Secret Midge was developed in the late 1990s, its name coined from a casual streamside joke with my friend and guide buddy Mick Stefan on a trip to the South Platte. The day was young, yet some midges were hatching, and I had already hooked a handful of fish in a tiny slot funneling into a beautiful run adjacent to the cliff-face hole in Trumbull. A pod of good fish were keying on pupae right below the surface, and it seemed like I could do no wrong by dead-drifting a tiny variegated brown midge right to them. It was a beautiful November day, and the fish were feeding heavily, fattening up and preparing for the leaner times that lay ahead.

After a while, my buddy couldn't take it anymore, and he yelled from downstream, "What are you using?"

"It's top secret. I can't tell you!" I said.

The air went silent, and then in a few seconds Stefan said, "C'mon man, what are you using?"

Of course, I was only kidding. This was a concoction that I had not named yet. I waved Stefan upstream, showed him what pattern I was using, and gave him a half-dozen. He went downstream twenty-five yards and immediately hooked a fish.

From that point on, this tiny midge was named the Top Secret Midge.

I frequently find myself fishing sizes 24-26 to fool the super-selective feeders that reside at Spinney Mountain Ranch, Elevenmile Canyon, and the Deckers/Cheesman stretches. The difference between fishing a #24 or #26 compared to a #20 is the difference between catching a few fish and not catching fish at all during the winter. From November through March, the

*The Top Secret Midge is the ultimate midge pattern. It's realistic, durable, easy to tie, and consistently fools hard-fished trout.*
JAY NICHOLS

*My favorite sizes of the Top Secret Midges (middle row) are #24 and #26.*

*Glamour Madera is synthetic embroidery thread that works perfectly for emerging wings on tiny midges and mayflies. It can be purchased from your local sewing shop.*

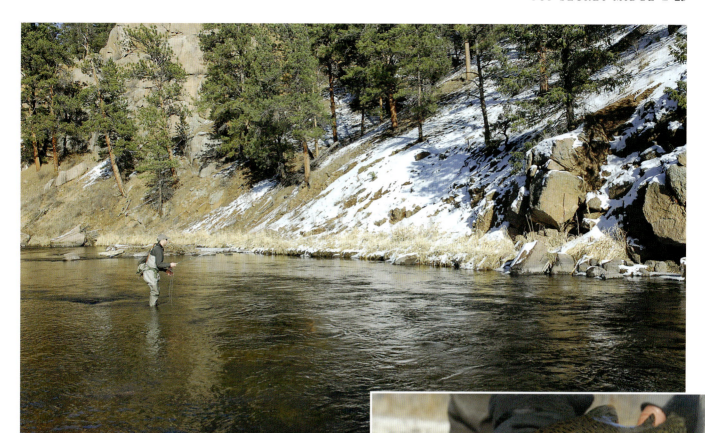

Cody Scott sight-fishes to a pod of South Platte trout with a Top Secret Midge, one of his favorite midge patterns in and around the Deckers area during the winter.

Midge feeders eat the Top Secret Midge with confidence. This rainbow took a Top Secret Midge dropped off a Nuclear Egg.

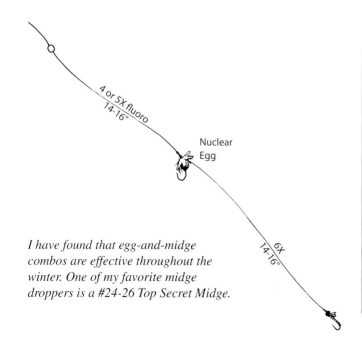

4 or 5X fluoro
14-16"

Nuclear Egg

6X
14-16"

I have found that egg-and-midge combos are effective throughout the winter. One of my favorite midge droppers is a #24-26 Top Secret Midge.

Top Secret Midge is my ace-in-the-hole pattern whenever fish are keying on microscopic midges. It has a two-color thread body that looks like a quill body but is much more durable, and the Glamour Madera wing has a brilliant flash when it twists and tumbles through the water column. By combining these materials, you have a realistic looking midge with adequate flash to simulate the gases in the pupa's thorax before it emerges.

**RIGGING AND FISHING TIPS**
In the winter, I typically try to target the slow, deep pools where trout congregate to conserve energy. The water temperatures are generally in the high 30s and low 40s, resulting in difficult fishing at best. The fish will feed for only a few hours each day, and at this time of year you hope that a good midge hatch will pull fish up into the shallow riffles to feed for a couple of hours so that you can capitalize on the opportunity.

# BUILDING YOUR OWN
# YARN INDICATOR

Most nymphing rigs on the streams that I fish consist of a strike indicator, two or three flies (check your local regulations for rules and regulations regarding the number of flies you can legally fish), and split-shot or tungsten putty. Anglers can choose from many strike indicators. Some prefer to use pinch-ons, cork and toothpick varieties, strike putty, yarn, Thingamabobbers, balloons, or pieces of Amnesia. Bar none, my favorite strike indicator is yarn because it is the most sensitive and makes it easiest to detect a strike. You can purchase premade yarn strike indicators or build your own. My preference is to build my own with a piece of craft cord and an orthodontist rubber band, which allows for easy adjustment. Thingamabobbers and balloons work well when it is windy, because they are easier to cast and cut a stiff breeze. Casting a piece of yarn in heavy wind is often problematic, and more times than not becomes more trouble than it's worth. Thingamabobbers and balloons, however, are not as sensitive to a strike, which can result in fewer fish. Thingamabobbers also hit the water hard, which may result in spooking trout that are suspended in the upper part of the water column feeding on midge pupae. I recommend carrying several types of indicators to use in different situations.

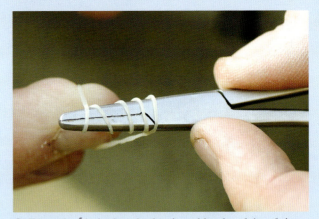

**2.** Wrap the 5/16-inch orthodontist rubber band 4 to 6 times around the tip of your hemostats. The number of wraps is determined by the thickness of the leader and where you will place the indicator. It takes more wraps to keep the strike indicator in place as the leader tapers in diameter.

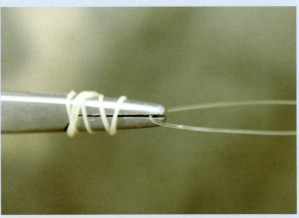

**3.** Form a U-shaped loop by pinching the leader with your index finger and thumb. Open the tip of your hemostats and grab the leader.

**1.** Purchase a bag of 5/16-inch orthodontist rubber bands and keep them in a plastic container. Grab one of the rubber bands with your index finger and thumb to begin building your own strike indicator.

**4.** Slide the rubber band off the tip of the hemostats onto the leader.

**5.** Open the loop with your index finger.

**6.** I use a three-strand polypropylene craft cord for my strike indicators. Separate and insert two strands of yarn (1½ inches long) into the loop and snug the rubber band into place.

**7.** Fluff the yarn with Velcro wrapped on a wood dowel.

**8.** Apply a modest amount of paste dry-fly floatant to the Velcro. My floatant of choice is Loon's Aquel.

**9.** Gently massage the paste floatant into the yarn. Refluff the yarn as needed and occasionally reapply floatant whenever the yarn begins to absorb water and sink.

I typically dredge this fly in the back end of the pool or deep slots. I try to avoid the faster water and keep focused on the slow-water stretches, plunge pools, and tailouts of the run. When a midge hatch becomes evident, and I see adults buzzing around the air, I begin to work the shallow riffles. I'll typically drop my Top Secret on 6X or 7X tippet off an egg pattern or another bright, flashy midge to draw attention to it.

It's hard to go wrong with an egg-and-midge combo throughout the winter. Fish that have fed on eggs from fall-spawning fish remember their high-protein diet. Also, the brightly colored patterns trigger strikes from fish that become aggressive before spawning in the spring. I still get more strikes on the Top Secret Midge, but the egg serves as a good attractor.

## Top Secret Midge

| Hook: | #18-26 Tiemco 2488 |
|---|---|
| Thread: | Brown 8/0 Uni-Thread |
| Abdomen: | Brown 8/0 Uni-Thread |
| Rib: | White 6/0 Uni-Thread |
| Wing: | Glamour Madera (#2400) |
| Thorax: | Rust-brown Superfine |

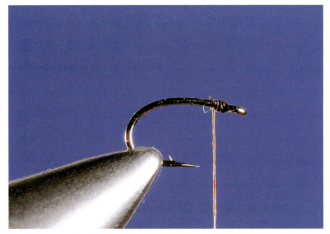

**1.** Place the hook in your vise and attach the thread behind the hook eye.

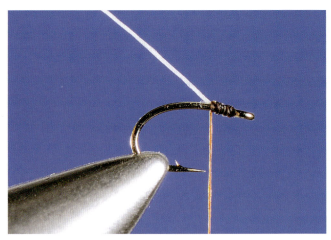

**2.** Cut a 6-inch piece of white thread from your bobbin and tie it in on top of the shank behind the hook eye. Use a new piece of white thread for each new fly; used thread tends to flare and will not look as clean.

**3.** Wrap the brown thread over the ribbing, one thread width at a time (keeping the ribbing on top of the hook shank), back toward the hook bend to form a smooth, even abdomen. Wrap the thread and ribbing a third of the way down the hook bend.

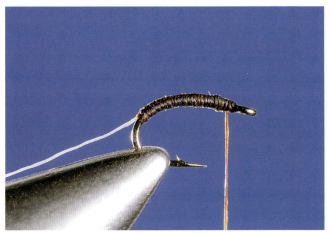

**4.** Wrap the thread forward one thread width at a time and leave it behind the hook eye.

**5.** Wrap the ribbing forward (do not reverse rib) toward the hook eye. Leave about one thread width between each wrap to create a segmented body.

**6.** Tie off the ribbing with four tight wraps of thread and clip it.

**7.** To simulate an emerging wing, tie in one strand of Glamour Madera at the point shown above with four tight wraps of thread. Leave the thread hanging in front of the Glamour Madera.

**8.** Using rust-brown Superfine, dub a football-shaped thorax in front of the wing.

**9.** Secure the dubbed thorax with four tight wraps of thread behind the hook eye.

**10.** Whip-finish and clip the thread.

**11.** Using your material hand, grab the Glamour Madera with your index finger and thumb and pull it forward to prop the wing up.

**12.** Hold the wing with your material hand's index finger and thumb and trim the emerging wing to size.

**13.** The length of the wing should be equivalent to one hook gap.

**14.** Fluff out the Glamour Madera with your index finger to produce a full wing.

**15.** This is how the wing should look after it has been combed out with your index finger.

**16.** Note how the abdomen is evenly segmented with two different colors of thread. The emerging wing should be full and the fly should have a tightly dubbed football-shaped thorax.

# CHAPTER 5

# *Medallion Midge Pupa*

Most midge patterns are impressionistic, tied with only a handful of materials: wire, thread, or Krystal Flash and a piece of tightly dubbed fur or wound peacock to imitate the bulbous thorax. These concoctions are designed with the fly tier in mind—they're easy to tie, durable, and consistently fool trout where midges abound. I designed the Medallion Midge Pupa, on the other hand, with selective trout in mind. The Medallion Midge takes the tying process a few steps further to produce a more realistic midge pupa. The abdomen is constructed like that of the Top Secret Midge, using two different colors of thread, producing a beautiful, extremely durable segmented body.

The thorax is constructed from Shane Stalcup's Medallion Sheeting, from which the fly takes its name. Medallion Sheeting comes in several colors—such as black, olive, brown, and dun—that make pattern variations as simple as changing colors of the thread abdomen and Medallion Sheeting. Medallion Sheeting produces a realistic looking thorax with a brilliant luster and backswept wing buds. Air bubbles get trapped between the dubbed thorax and wing buds, producing an imitation of the gas bubble that forms on the naturals.

## RIGGING AND FISHING TIPS

The Medallion Midge Pupa is most effective dead-drifted with a conventional strike indicator and a small shot. Once trout are eating midge pupae selectively, I typically fish this pattern with another midge pupa like a Mercury Black Beauty, being careful to manage my weight to ensure my flies are in the trout's feeding zone.

If I notice the fish are becoming sensitive to a standard two-fly nymphing rig, I'll drop a Medallion Midge off a heavily hackled Griffith's Gnat. Carefully analyze where the trout are

*The Medallion Midge Pupa is one of the most realistic pupa patterns that I have ever fished.* JAY NICHOLS

By changing the color of the thread in the abdomen, you can tie black, brown, and chartreuse variations of the Medallion Midge. The 6/0 white thread is the common denominator to all the variations. JAY NICHOLS

Bob Dye plays a hard-fighting Gray Reef rainbow that he fooled on a Medallion Midge below Alcova Dam. The Medallion Midge has become a local favorite for guides and fisherman alike.

# IN THE ZONE

The old adage "The difference between a good fisherman and a great fisherman is one split-shot" is not far from the truth. You can have the right fly, but if you don't fish it in the right feeding zone, you won't catch any fish.

Through careful observation, you should be able to make an educated guess as to which part of the water column the trout are holding in. Your first consideration should be whether or not the fish you spot are feeding. Are they hugging the bottom, mid-column, or finning a few inches below the surface? Feeding fish are not difficult to fool, but non-feeding fish are almost impossible to get to eat. I try to concentrate my efforts on finding actively feeding trout that are often suspended in the water column. I make it a point to ignore the non-feeders hugging the bottom of the river.

The density of the hatch determines whether or not the trout will be actively feeding and where the trout will be holding in the water column. If the hatches are sporadic, the trout will generally sit near the bottom. Sporadic hatches result in very little feeding activity. If there is a good hatch, the trout will be suspended in the water column and actively feed. If there is a heavy hatch, they will move into prime feeding lies such as shallow riffles, mid-channel shelves, and gravel bars. It's rare to see a trout in shallow riffles unless there is a strong hatch where the abundance of food outweighs the risk of predators.

To keep your flies in the right feeding zone, you must constantly manage your strike indicator and weight. Each riffle, run, pool, slot, or transitional zone has its own set of requirements. Do not be lazy in adjusting your weight—otherwise you may cost yourself strikes in the long run.

As the hatch intensifies and trout move into the shallow riffles and transitional zones (mid-channel shelves and gravel bars), less weight is necessary. To reduce the

*This Williams Fork brown trout took a Medallion Midge during a heavy midge hatch.* JAY NICHOLS

weight, which in theory raises your flies in the water column, simply remove part of the Mojo Mud or other putty and stick it back on your lanyard or zipper pull. Adjust your strike indicator accordingly—keeping it 1½ to 2 times the depth of the feeding fish from your flies.

During the height of the hatch, you may only need the split-shot. Actively feeding fish will be higher in the water column and will move several inches to eat swimming *Baetis* or suspended midge pupa. It is entirely possible that your weight and strike indicator may be only 12 to 18 inches apart. As the hatch starts to slow down, you'll need to begin adding weight and moving your strike indicator to achieve the same goals by lowering your flies in the water column.

suspended in the water column, as this will help you determine how much tippet you'll need on your dropper. In most cases, 18 to 24 inches of tippet is ideal for fooling trout feeding on midge pupae in the upper part of the water column. I typically attach a micro shot about 6 inches above the unweighted Medallion Midge to keep it in this zone.

If I see trout feeding on midges with headless, back-to-tail rises, they are typically feeding on pupae in the surface film, and I fish the Medallion Midge with the greased-leader technique, suspending the fly just below the meniscus. To imitate the pupa hanging vertically below the surface, dress your leader with a paste floatant, leaving the last 12 inches closest to the fly untreated. The upper part of the leader will sit on the

surface, while the weight of the undressed leader and fly will allow the pupa to sit flush or slightly below the film. Cast your fly directly upstream, carefully watching the water for any surface disturbance, and set the hook if you see a back roll in the general vicinity of your fly. You must be precise with your delivery because the trout's cone of vision is very small when they are suspended in the upper part of the water column. Because the fish are suspended directly below the surface, they will be extremely spooky. Sneaking in from behind your target or kneeling down to reduce the height of your silhouette decreases the chances of spooking it. You may need to crawl on your hands and knees under these circumstances.

### Medallion Midge Pupa

| | |
|---|---|
| Hook: | #18-24 Tiemco 101 |
| Thread: | Dark-brown 8/0 Uni-Thread |
| Abdomen: | Dark-brown 8/0 Uni-Thread |
| Rib: | White 6/0 Uni-Thread |
| Thorax: | Rust-brown Superfine |
| Wing Buds: | Medium-dun Medallion Sheeting |

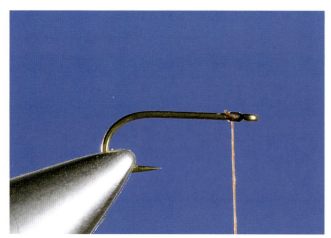

**1.** Place the hook in your vise and attach the thread behind the hook eye.

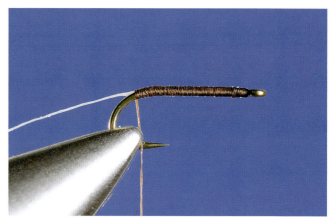

**2.** Tie in a 6-inch piece of white 6/0 Uni-Thread thread behind the hook eye. Wrap the brown thread back toward the hook bend over the white thread. Keep the wraps symmetrical, making sure none of the white thread is exposed. Use a new piece of white thread for each new fly, otherwise the thread will flare and the rib will not look as clean.

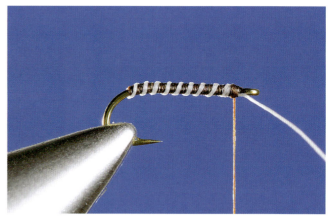

**3.** Palmer the rib forward. To keep the thread from flaring, I do not reverse-rib this pattern. The spacing between each rib should be equivalent to the diameter of the white thread. Tie off the ribbing with four tight wraps of thread.

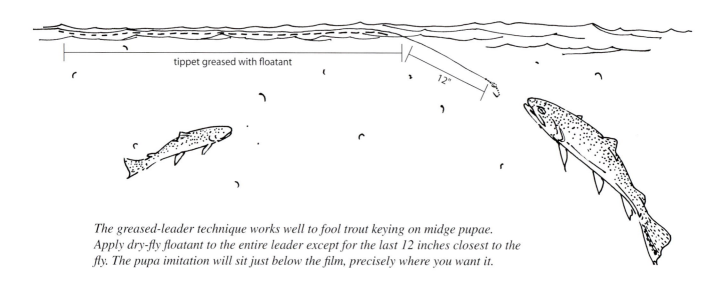

tippet greased with floatant

12"

*The greased-leader technique works well to fool trout keying on midge pupae. Apply dry-fly floatant to the entire leader except for the last 12 inches closest to the fly. The pupa imitation will sit just below the film, precisely where you want it.*

**4.** The thorax area, wing case, and wing buds are tied from medium dun Medallion Sheeting.

**5.** Using a self-healing cutting mat, rotary cutter, and straight edge, cut the Medallion Sheeting into strips.

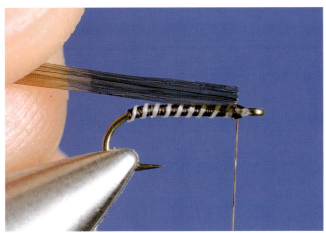

**6.** The width of the Medallion Sheeting should be about half of the hook gap. Cut several strips at a time to save time in the tying process.

**7.** Tie in the Medallion Sheeting behind the hook eye with four tight wraps of thread. The Medallion Sheeting should be on top of the hook shank.

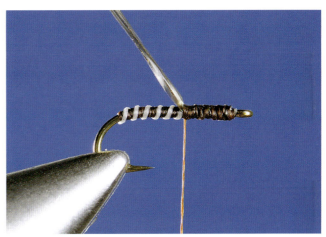

**8.** Wrap the thread back toward the middle of the hook shank, covering the Medallion Sheeting. Leave the thread at the midpoint of the hook shank.

**9.** Lay a separate piece of Medallion Sheeting (¾ of a hook gap) across the hook shank. Tie it in with an X pattern, consisting of three tight wraps in each direction.

**10.** After you have secured the Medallion Sheeting, leave the thread hanging slightly in front of the tie-in point. The Medallion Sheeting should be at a 90-degree angle to the hook shank.

**11.** With your thumb and index finger, pull the Medallion Sheeting straight back over the hook shank.

**12.** Hold the Medallion Sheeting with your thumb and index finger. Make four tight wraps of thread to secure it.

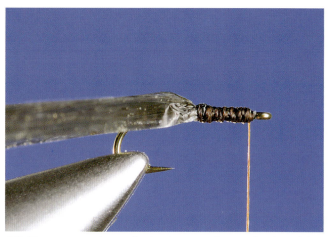

**13.** Even out any lumps in the thorax and wrap the thread forward to the hook eye.

**14.** Form a thin and sparse dubbing noodle with rust-brown Superfine.

**15.** Dub the thorax back to the three strips of Medallion Sheeting.

**16.** Wrap the dubbing noodle back toward the hook eye, producing a football-like taper. If there is any additional dubbing, remove it, and make four tight wraps of thread behind the eye. Be careful not to crowd the head.

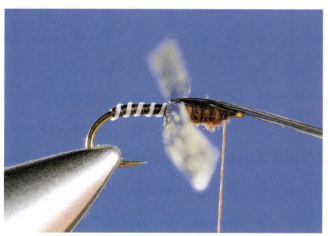

**17.** Pull the strip of Medallion Sheeting on top of the hook shank over the dubbed thorax.

**18.** Make two tight thread wraps to secure the Medallion Sheeting. Trim the end of the Medallion Sheeting as close to the thread as possible.

**19.** Pull the two remaining strips of Medallion Sheeting forward so that they run parallel along the side of the thorax.

**20.** Make two tight turns of thread to secure the Medallion Sheeting. Do not cut the butt ends, as they will be used to form the wing buds.

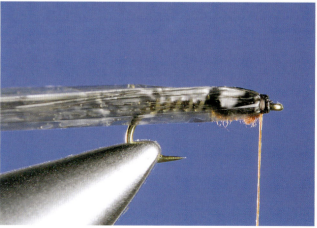

**21.** With your thumb and index finger, pull the Medallion Sheeting back toward the hook bend. The Medallion Sheeting should run parallel to the hook shank. Make two tight wraps to secure it.

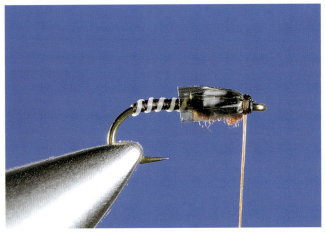

**22.** Trim the Medallion Sheeting on each side of the thorax. Cut each side separately. The wing buds should extend slightly beyond the dubbed thorax.

**23.** With a sharp pair of scissors, round off the Medallion Sheeting to create lifelike wing buds.

**24.** Whip-finish the head.

**25.** The thread abdomen should be uniformly segmented between the hook bend and the thorax. The tightly dubbed thorax should be football-shaped with the wing buds one-third the overall length of the fly and extending slightly beyond the dubbing.

**26.** Top view of finished fly.

# CHAPTER 6

# *Mercury Brassie*

Gene Lynch, Ken Chandler, and Tug Davenport, veteran South Platte anglers and passionate fly tiers, carved their way into angling history by developing one of the best midge patterns ever plucked from a trout's jaw. During one of their tying sessions, they came up with the idea of wrapping copper wire around a hook shank to give their standard nymphs a quicker sink rate. This was in the 1960s when there were no bead-heads, tungsten underbodies, or moldable putty weights.

According to Bill Chandler, son of Ken Chandler, the discovery of the Brassie was really an accident. Somehow one of weighted flies became worn and tattered, exposing the shiny, copper wire underbody. To their surprise, the trout ate it like it was going out of style. With that in mind, Lynch, Chandler, and

Davenport took one of their copper wire underbodies and added a small piece of black heat-shrink tubing for the head and called their new innovation the South Platte Brassie.

According to Ed Engle in *Tying Small Flies*, "As the word got around about the effectiveness of the Brassie, innovative tiers began using enameled wire stripped from old motor armatures and transformers." There was only one problem, however: "Tiers who cranked out a season's supply over the winter found that the bright, shiny copper wire oxidized within a month or so, and the flies became ineffective."

The Brassie become so popular in the 1960s that Lynch, Chandler, and Davenport marketed them. Engle further notes that Brassies that were sold in the 1960s were placed in gelatin

*The Mercury Brassie is a variation of the original Brassie developed by Gene Lynch, Ken Chandler, and Tug Davenport. The original Brassie and its variations have been South Platte favorites for decades.* JAY NICHOLS

39

*I tie my Mercury Brassies in a wide range of colors and sizes. My favorites include red, black, and blue in sizes 18-22.*
JAY NICHOLS

# DRY-AND-DROPPER RIGS

As runoff begins to recede, many of the previously hard-to-get-to spots become likely holding spots for trout. This is a great time of the year to carry two rods—one set up with a dry-and-dropper rig to fish pocketwater and shallow riffles and runs, and one set up with a conventional two-fly nymphing rig for the deeper holes. I'll often fish an area with a dry-and-dropper rig and then fish it with my nymphing rig to cover the entire water column.

When trout become suspicious of standard two-fly nymphing rigs, fishing a dry fly and a dropper enables you to cover a wide assortment of water, including transitional zones that funnel into deep pools, riffles, runs, pockets, bank water, and protruding logs. This rig works especially well in shallow water that rarely gets fished with a conventional nymphing rig.

Your dry fly can be an attractor or selected to match the hatch. For instance, if caddis are hatching, I'll use a caddis; if Golden Stones are hatching, I'll use an Amy's Ant, and so on. I typically choose my bead-head dropper with the same thought in mind. If midges are hatching, I'll use a Mercury Brassie, Zebra Midge, or Bead-Head Black Beauty. If mayflies are moving, I use a Bead-Head Barr Emerger, Mercer's Micro Mayfly, or Bead-Head Pheasant Tail. If you are looking for a quicker sink rate, use flies with tungsten beads.

Dry-and-dropper rigs can also be effective throughout the winter, but you'll need to tweak your tactics to match the prevailing conditions. Throughout the winter, I'll typically fish with a #18-20 Parachute Adams or Griffith's Gnat dropped with a midge pupa. Treat your dry fly with Aquel or Frog's Fanny so that it rides high on the surface of the water. If your fly becomes waterlogged, you'll miss subtle strikes.

This tactic is especially effective on rivers like the Bighorn where you see heavy concentrations of midges or midge clusters. I have run across many cases in back channels where the trout are feeding sporadically on adults and keying heavily on pupae. Fish suspended below the current, moving 3 or 4 inches to either side to eat, are typically feeding on emerging midge pupae. The inclination is to fish a dry fly once you see rising fish, but keep in mind the fish are eating a lot more pupae than adults during the initial phases of the hatch. With this approach, you're covering your bases, and fish will eat your adult imitation from time to time; more often than not, however, they will eat the dropper. Fish in skinny water will quit feeding if you plop a strike indicator and a bunch of lead on their heads. The dry-and-dropper approach will not spook as many trout. Once the trout become fully engaged on the adults, I'll cut off the dropper fly and fish one or two dry flies. From my past experiences, once trout commit to the adult, they begin feeding selectively and ignore the pupae.

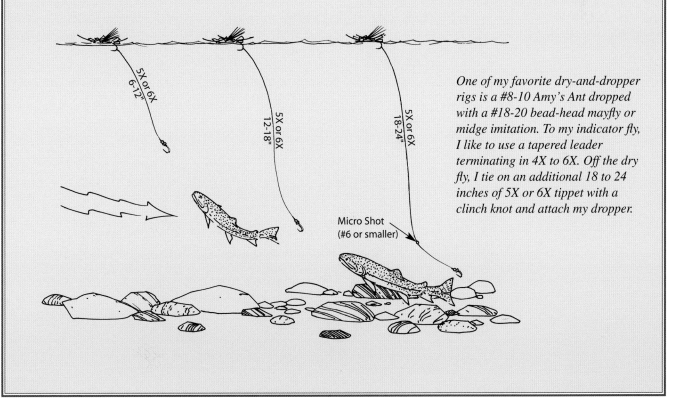

*One of my favorite dry-and-dropper rigs is a #8-10 Amy's Ant dropped with a #18-20 bead-head mayfly or midge imitation. To my indicator fly, I like to use a tapered leader terminating in 4X to 6X. Off the dry fly, I tie on an additional 18 to 24 inches of 5X or 6X tippet with a clinch knot and attach my dropper.*

5X or 6X
6-12"

5X or 6X
12-18"

5X or 6X
18-24"

Micro Shot
(#6 or smaller)

*Wade Brand fishes with a Mercury Brassie above "the wall" in the upper part of Cheesman Canyon. The Mercury Brassie has proven to be an excellent attractor in a two-fly nymphing rig.*

capsules to keep them from oxidizing. Single flies were placed in gelatin capsules and hung on a card for display. Copper, red, and green were the most popular colors. They imitated the most common colors of midge larvae and pupae found along the South Platte watershed.

In the 1970s fly tiers began buying spooled wire in fly shops because it did not oxidize and stayed as shiny as on the day it was purchased. The fly-shop copper wire was treated with clear polyurethane and a nylon overcoat to keep it from oxidizing. In

the mid-1970s, anglers began using peacock herl, dubbing, or wound thread for the head, which is still the norm today.

The Mercury Brassie, an offshoot of the original that uses peacock for the thorax and a silver-lined glass bead, fishes well on almost any drainage because it imitates midge larvae and pupae. If you change the color and tie it in larger sizes (#14-16), it also imitates caddis larvae. The weight of the Ultra Wire helps keep the fly bouncing along the bottom where the biggest concentrations of trout are found. You can tie it in a wide range

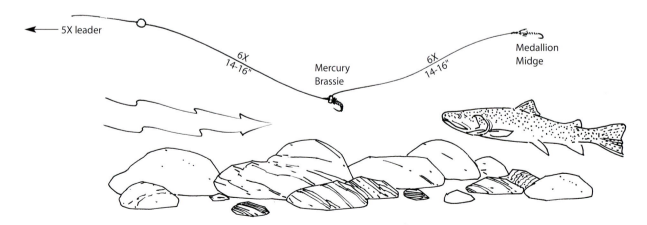

*Fishing the combination of a heavier nymph like the Mercury Brassie and a buoyant pupa like the Medallion Midge is an effective strategy for imitating midge larvae near the substrate and pupae that are just beginning to emerge.*

of colors, including copper, red, chartreuse, blue, silver, green, and black. My favorite colors are copper, black, red, and blue, which is an especially effective color when the light is low.

## RIGGING AND FISHING TIPS

I typically use the Mercury Brassie as the attractor in a two-fly nymphing rig, dropping another small midge or mayfly nymph off it. Effective droppers include #18-22 Mercury Flashback Pheasant Tails, Sparkle Wing RS2s, Barr Emergers (BWO and PMD), Juju Baetis, Mercury Black Beauties, Jujubee Midges, and Top Secret Midges.

The Mercury Brassie is also great choice for dry-and-dropper rigs. When nothing is hatching, I'll typically fish a Mercury Brassie below a Stimulator, Limeade, Elk-Hair Caddis, Puterbaugh Caddis, or Amy's Ant. It is especially effective in water that is about a foot deep. If I'm fishing deeper water, I often lengthen the distance between my flies and add a micro shot (size 6 or smaller) inches above my fly.

### Mercury Brassie

| | |
|---|---|
| Hook: | #14-24 Tiemco 2487 |
| Bead: | Clear, silver-lined glass bead (extra small) |
| Thread: | Black 8/0 Uni-Thread |
| Abdomen: | Copper Ultra Wire |
| Thorax: | Peacock herl |
| Note: | Use medium Ultra Wire for #14-16, brassie for #18-20, and small for #22-24. |

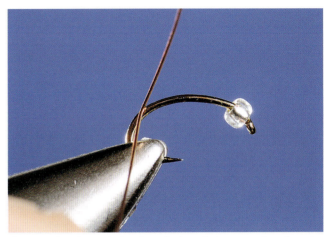

**1.** Put a bead on the hook and place it in your vise. Spool a bobbin with copper wire, pull out 6 inches, and lay the wire across the shank.

*This rainbow was fooled with a red Mercury Brassie on the North Fork of the South Platte River near Shawnee, Colorado.*

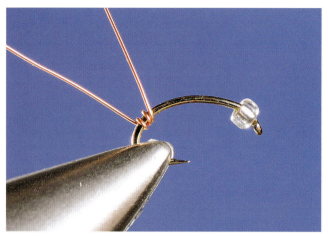

**2.** Hold on to the copper wire with your left hand while wrapping the remaining piece clockwise up the hook shank. This technique alleviates any unnecessary bulk that arises from tying the wire in near the hook eye and running it to the rear of the shank before wrapping it forward.

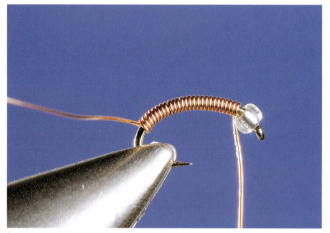

**3.** Wrap the wire up the hook shank to the glass bead, making sure the wire is tight and symmetrical.

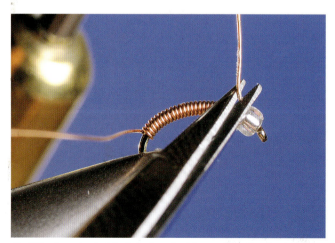

**4.** Clip the wire behind the bead with an old pair of scissors as close to the hook shank as possible.

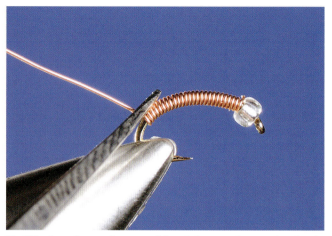

**5.** Clip the wire on the rear of the abdomen close to the shank.

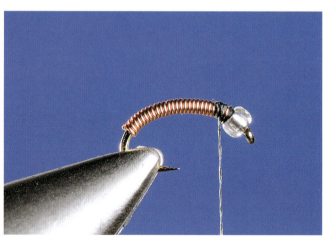

**6.** Attach the thread with a jam knot behind the bead. Secure the copper wire behind the bead with several wraps of thread. Make sure that a couple of the wraps go between the copper wire, firmly securing the abdomen to the hook shank.

**7.** Tie in a piece of peacock herl (from the eye) tip first to be used for the collar. The tip of the peacock eye is not as brittle as the butt end, so tying it tip first reduces the risk of any breakage.

**8.** Wrap the peacock herl forward, making seven clockwise turns to produce a full collar. Tie off and secure the peacock herl with four wraps of thread.

**9.** Trim the butt end of the peacock herl. Take four wraps of thread between the collar and bead to produce a smooth band of thread.

**10.** Whip-finish and clip thread. I do not use head cement on this fly, as it tends to ruin the peacock herl.

**11.** The finished Mercury Brassie. Its streamlined shape makes it an excellent choice for a dropper fly.

## *Mercury Brassie (Red)*

| | |
|---|---|
| Hook: | #14-24 Tiemco 2487 |
| Bead: | Clear, silver-lined glass bead (extra small) |
| Thread: | Black 8/0 Uni-Thread |
| Abdomen: | Red Ultra Wire |
| Thorax: | Peacock herl |

Note: Use medium Ultra Wire for #14-16, brassie for #18-20, and small for #22-24.

### Mercury Brassie (Chartreuse)

Hook:         #14-24 Tiemco 2487
Bead:         Clear, silver-lined glass bead (extra small)
Thread:       Black 8/0 Uni-Thread
Abdomen:      Chartreuse Ultra Wire
Thorax:       Peacock herl

Note: Use medium Ultra Wire for #14-16, brassie for #18-20, and small for #22-24.

### Mercury Brassie (Black)

Hook:         #14-24 Tiemco 2487
Bead:         Clear, silver-lined glass bead (extra small)
Thread:       Black 8/0 Uni-Thread
Abdomen:      Black Ultra Wire
Thorax:       Peacock herl

Note: Use medium Ultra Wire for #14-16, brassie for #18-20, and small for #22-24.

### Mercury Brassie (Blue)

Hook:         #14-24 Tiemco 2487
Bead:         Clear, silver-lined glass bead (extra small)
Thread:       Black 8/0 Uni-Thread
Abdomen:      Royal-blue Ultra Wire
Thorax:       Peacock herl

Note: Use medium Ultra Wire for #14-16, brassie for #18-20, and small for #22-24,

### Mercury Brassie (Green)

Hook:         #14-24 Tiemco 2487
Bead:         Clear, silver-lined glass bead (extra small)
Thread:       Black 8/0 Uni-Thread
Abdomen:      Green Ultra Wire
Thorax:       Peacock herl

Note: Use medium Ultra Wire for #14-16, brassie for #18-20, and small for #22-24.

# CHAPTER 7

# Hi-Viz Griffith's Gnat

Y ou'd be hard-pressed to find a more versatile midge pattern than the Griffith's Gnat. Invented by George Griffith in the late 1960s, it was originally designed to imitate the stage between the emerging pupa and the adult. I most often use the Griffith's Gnat to imitate individual adult midges in sizes 20-26.

There is nothing more exciting, or challenging, than finding a pod of rising fish keying on adult midges. Midges have an aversion to bright sunlight; therefore the best hatches tend to be in low light conditions. Early morning before the sun hits the water is good, and when the sun begins to dip behind the canyon wall around 5 PM, the river can come alive with trout dimpling the surface as they take midges.

Midge feeders generally suspend below the surface, so the feeding window is only a few inches in diameter, and a cast that is a few inches to the left or right is often not good enough to fool them. Toss in cruising trout, and things become really challenging. In all situations, target specific rising fish rather than flock-shooting. If you are not casting to a specific fish, your odds go down dramatically.

Under normal conditions, the best midge hatches occur during the last two hours before dark. In most cases, this means fishing tiny dry flies (#22-26) with 7X tippet to imitate single adult midges. The Griffith's Gnat is hard to see, especially in the evening, when surface glare makes dry-fly fishing extremely challenging. A Hi-Viz Griffith's Gnat helps solve this problem.

*This butterball 20-inch rainbow took a Hi-Viz Griffith's Gnat during a midge hatch. The Hi-Viz Griffith's Gnat is easy to see in smaller sizes, especially in scum lines and heavy glare.* JAY NICHOLS

*This Taylor River brown took a Griffith's Gnat during a heavy midge emergence. Contrary to what many anglers believe, the Hog Trough has very reliable midge hatches with a lot of rising fish.*
JAY NICHOLS

*The Griffith's Gnat is a versatile midge pattern because it can be fished as a small midge cluster or an individual midge. Midge clusters are common on many tailwaters. This cluster of midges congregated on the side of my drift boat while fishing the Bighorn River near Fort Smith, Montana.*

It is similar to a standard Griffith's Gnat, but it has a brightly colored (fluorescent pink, orange, or chartreuse) McFlylon post that makes the fly stand out in foam mats, bubble lines, riffled seams, and evening glare. To make it even easier to see, apply Frog's Fanny or Dry Shake to the fly to turn the top white.

I also use a #14-18 Griffith's Gnat to imitate clusters of midges, which are common on Western tailwaters, such as the Bighorn in southern Montana and the San Juan in northern New Mexico. Clusters of midges the size of a Frisbee are a common sight in the shade or during low light conditions.

I have had incredible dry-fly fishing in the back channels with large Griffith's Gnats when midge clusters were congregating in the slower water, back eddies, and tailouts. Small chunks of adult midges (the size of a piece of popcorn) often separate themselves from the main clump and become a hearty meal for opportunistic trout. I have sat in amazement watching a trout rise up and consume a small cluster of adult midges. I carry some larger #12 Griffith's Gnats in case I encounter this situation.

## RIGGING AND FISHING TIPS

My conventional dry-fly setup incorporates a 9-foot leader, to which I add 18 to 24 inches of 5X (on #10-14 flies) or 5X to 7X (on #16-24 flies). I almost always use 7X with flies below #20—necessary with flies this small, though you'll occasionally break off a nice fish or two.

I like to stack the deck in my favor, so when fishing midges, I not only use a highly visible pattern treated with Frog's Fanny, but I also fish it behind another pattern such as a Parachute Adams or small Hi-Viz Baetis. In a two-fly rig, I typically space my flies 14 to 16 inches apart, with the point fly tied off the bend of the upper fly. If you cannot see your Griffith's Gnat, set the hook to any swirl within a 2-foot distance of your Parachute Adams or Hi-Viz Baetis. This rig is especially effective in foam line or scum lines.

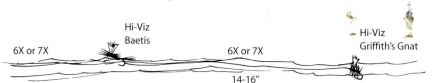

*A Hi-Viz Baetis and a Hi-Viz Griffith's Gnat give you the edge you need when fishing small flies.*

## Hi-Viz Griffith's Gnat

| | |
|---|---|
| Hook: | #14-26 Tiemco 101 |
| Thread: | Black 8/0 Uni-Thread |
| Abdomen: | Peacock herl (eye) |
| Post: | Fluorescent-pink McFlylon |
| Hackle: | Grizzly rooster |

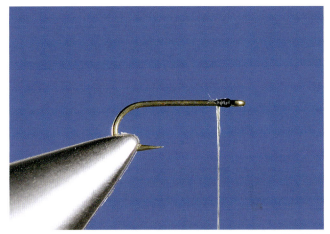

**1.** Place the hook into your vise and attach the thread behind the hook eye.

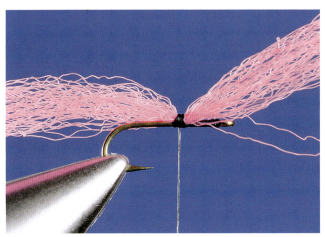

**2.** Wrap the thread back from the eye one hook gap. In doing so, develop a uniform thread base along the hook shank. Tie in a strand of McFlylon along the hook shank with six tight wraps of thread. The thickness of the post will vary depending on the size of the fly. On larger Griffith's Gnats (#16-18) I use a full strand of McFlylon and remove a few fibers from the post as I progress smaller in size.

**3.** Clip the butt ends of McFlylon at a 45-degree angle to the hook shank. The remaining piece of McFlylon should extend past the hook eye.

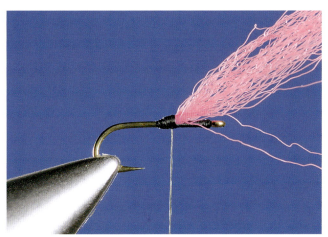

**4.** With several tight wraps of thread, secure the butt ends of the McFlylon. Smooth out the taper with thread, trying to minimize the angle between the post and hook shank.

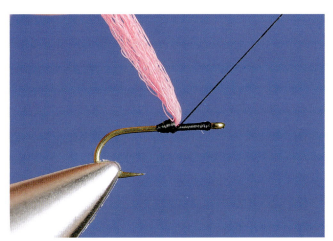

**5.** With your left index finger and thumb, pull the McFlylon back at a slight angle and form a thread wedge in front of the post to hold it in place.

**6.** Make several wraps of thread in front of the McFlylon to prop the post up. Smooth out the taper in front of the post with thread.

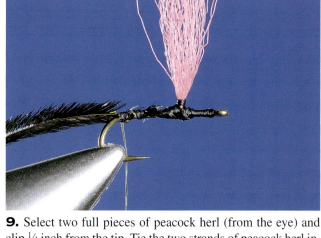

**9.** Select two full pieces of peacock herl (from the eye) and clip ¼ inch from the tip. Tie the two strands of peacock herl in, tip first.

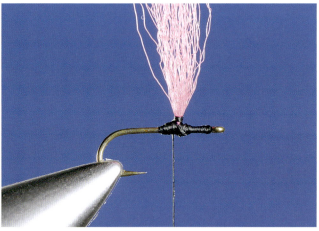

**7.** Wrap the thread several times clockwise around the base of the post to hold the McFlylon fibers together. Make two tight wraps of thread around the hook shank behind the post to secure it upright.

**10.** Select the proper size grizzly hackle. I like Whiting Farms 100 packs. Strip one hook gap-length of the barbules off the butt end of the hackle, exposing the center quill.

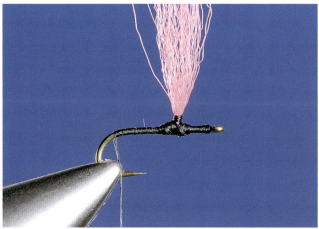

**8.** Wrap the thread back toward the hook bend. Create a smooth thread base between the rear of the post and the hook bend.

**11.** Tie the hackle in with the dull side up with four tight wraps of thread. Leave a small section of the quill exposed beyond the hook bend.

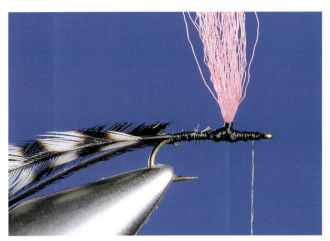

**12.** Wrap the thread forward to the hook eye. Smooth out any rough areas in the thread base.

**13.** With your index finger and thumb, wrap the two strips of peacock herl forward. Each consecutive wrap should be in front of the previous one to avoid matted-down peacock herl. Tie off the peacock herl behind the hook eye with two tight wraps of thread.

**14.** Grab the hackle with your index finger and thumb and palmer the hackle forward. You may use hackle pliers for this step, but I find that I have better control with my hands. I generally make four to five turns of hackle between the hook bend and the post.

**15.** Continue wrapping the hackle toward the hook eye. Hold the hackle back at a slight angle to avoid trapping any barbules, and tie it off with four tight wraps of thread.

**16.** Trim the hackle as close to the head as possible. Remove any stray hackle fibers trapped by the thread.

**17.** Bury the butt end of the hackle with several wraps of thread. Clip the thread and whip-finish.

**18.** Trim the post to the desired length. On this pattern, I typically keep the post as large as, or slightly larger than, the hackle.

**20.** A conventional Griffith's Gnat without a post.

**19.** You must use two full pieces of peacock herl (selected from the peacock eye) for the body. In my opinion, a good Griffith's Gnat is a heavily hackled Griffith's Gnat. The McFlylon wing should be as high as, or slightly higher than, the hackle.

# CHAPTER 8

# Mercury Mayflies

Blue-Winged Olives (BWOs), Pale Morning Duns (PMDs), and *Tricorythodes* (Tricos) are the "big three" of tailwater and spring-creek mayflies, and the most prevalent of the big three mayflies is the Blue-Winged Olive, or *Baetis*. Several species are multi-brooded, typically hatching from mid March to early May and again from early September through late October. It is not uncommon to see sporadic duns through mid November. Because they can hatch in cold weather, at a time when there is little other mayfly activity, *Baetis* provide anglers with excellent nymph-fishing opportunities and reliable dry-fly fishing each afternoon between 1 and 3 PM on overcast days.

Beginning in late June, PMDs begin hatching as spring runoff begins to recede. The quality of dry-fly fishing hinges on water levels—if the river's flows are normal and moderately clear, anglers can expect to find some good surface activity. Before and during the hatch, fishing with nymphs and emergers can be very good in moderate-paced riffles.

Tricos become important mid to late summer, extending well into autumn. They too, are multi-brooded, producing reliable morning hatches between mid July and late October. Sporadic hatches may occur as early as late June or early July. Unlike Blue-Winged Olives and Pale Morning Duns, the Trico spinnerfall takes precedence over the duns, producing some of

*Between April and late October, I have a lot of confidence in my Mercury Mayflies. Two of my favorites are the Baetis and PMD versions.* JAY NICHOLS

53

the best dry-fly fishing of the season. While the trout eat the duns, they do not eat them as much as the spinners.

Over the years, Mercury Mayflies have been some of my clutch patterns before and during a hatch. They are especially effective on bright, sunny days when mayfly duns leave the water quickly and the trout strongly favor the nymphs.

## MERCURY BAETIS

*Baetis* nymphs, which have slender, dark olive-brown abdomens with darkened wing pads, thrive in weed-rich spring creeks and tailwaters. I incorporate black Z-lon into the Mercury Baetis' design to imitate the naturals' prominent pre-emergence wing

*Matt Miles spotted this brown trout sitting on the leading edge of a gravel bar during a Blue-Winged Olive hatch. The fish were ignoring duns, but they were keying heavily on* Baetis *nymphs. He fooled this trout with a #20 Mercury Baetis.*

pads. *Baetis* nymphs are also excellent swimmers, and imitating the natural behavior of the emerging nymph is as important as choosing the fly itself. Trout keying on *Baetis* nymphs tend to be suspended in the current and chase nymphs in an upward gliding fashion before returning to their holding position. Trout keying on midges only move a few inches to intercept a pupa, whereas trout eating swimming mayflies may move from several inches to a foot or more. Trout often key on the swimming *Baetis* and ignore the dead-drifted imposters. This is one case where dead-drifting your flies may limit your success, so be willing to change your tactics and experiment a bit. Special lifting or rising tactics such as the Leisenring Lift, or allowing your flies to swing prematurely in the current, can imitate this emerging behavior. During the peak of the hatch, trout may move as far as 18 inches to intercept an emerging *Baetis*. If you see a trout flash, lift, or chase something near your flies, set the hook.

*Baetis* nymph imitations work year-round; however, their greatest importance is just before and during spring and fall hatches. Some of the best nymph fishing of the year occurs with tiny *Baetis* nymphs. Autumn Blue-Winged Olives are one to two sizes smaller than the ones that hatch in the spring, so I carry *Baetis* nymphs and adults in sizes 18 to 24.

On bright, sunny days, I have seen the water completely covered with duns, yet no trout rising. Under these circumstances, when trout are keying on nymphs and emergers below the surface, a skilled nymph fisherman can do very well. If skies are overcast, trout tend to feed more on the surface. Despite knowing that the trout are still eating huge quantities of *Baetis* nymphs under the surface, I love dry-fly fishing so much, I typically switch tactics and begin fishing dry flies when I can see fish rising consistently. The best Blue-Winged Olive hatches occur during inclement weather. Some of the best hatches I've experienced have been during nasty spring snowstorms or when it has drizzled all day. In these conditions, the hatch will typically start around midday and last for three or four hours.

**EMERGING BAETIS RIG**

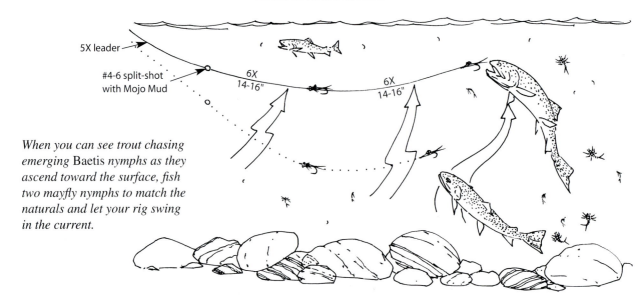

5X leader

#4-6 split-shot with Mojo Mud

6X 14-16"

6X 14-16"

*When you can see trout chasing emerging* Baetis *nymphs as they ascend toward the surface, fish two mayfly nymphs to match the naturals and let your rig swing in the current.*

## Rigging and Fishing Tips

During spring and autumn, I typically begin my day by fishing with a midge and mayfly nymph to match the prevalent food at that time of year. As I begin to see trout moving, shifting, and lifting in the water column midday—signs that trout are beginning to feed on *Baetis* emergers—I switch to two *Baetis* nymphs. As the hatch progresses, I pump the stomach of a fish to make sure that the pattern I am using is the right size, shape, and color.

I often fish a Mercury Baetis as my attractor and trail an emerging *Baetis* such as a Sparkle Wing RS2 or a Mercury Flashback RS2 from it. I use a conventional nymphing rig with an adjustable yarn strike indicator, keeping my flies spaced 14 to 16 inches apart, with my weight 14 to 16 inches above my upper fly. If the water is really clear and the fish are selective, I use 6X fluorocarbon.

## MERCURY PMD

As high water begins to recede, Pale Morning Duns (similar to Sulphurs in the eastern United States) become the prominent mayfly. Hatches may last from one to three or more weeks. Nymphs vary in color from pale or tannish brown to a dirty yellow. As summer progresses, the naturals become gradually smaller—by as much as one hook size. I typically fish a #18 pattern in June and the first two weeks of July and then switch to a #20 by late July and fish it through August. Since the Mercury PMD is tied on a 2X-long hook with a longer shank, you should fish one size smaller than the natural (a #18 to imitate a #16 natural).

A PMD nymph's underside is lighter than the top, so I use brown Z-lon for the wing pads and legs. PMD nymphs are considerably more robust in the thorax area than the streamlined *Baetis* nymphs, so add a little bit of extra dubbing to the thorax when you tie it.

PMD nymphs are crawlers and thrive in streams with a substrate comprised of smaller rocks, stones, and gravel. The nymphs prefer slow to medium currents, and after they hatch, the duns frequently float on the surface of glassy pools and tailouts. I typically fish a Mercury PMD methodically in transitional areas (mid-channel shelves and gravel bars) and shallow riffles that funnel into runs and occasionally in moderate-paced pocketwater. Since PMDs are feeble swimmers, trout do not feed on them as aggressively as they do when eating *Baetis* nymphs.

The timing of PMD hatches varies considerably depending on the drainage. They may hatch from 10 AM to noon or midday between 1 PM and 3 PM. If skies are overcast, expect a full-blown hatch with several rising trout. If it is bright and sunny, PMD nymphs generally work best.

## Rigging and Fishing Tips

I rig and fish PMDs the same way that I do *Baetis,* except that I use larger tippet (typically 5X fluorocarbon) for the larger

*Suzie Moskal nymphs a mid-channel shelf with a Mercury PMD in the middle of July. The South Platte River at Spinney Mountain Ranch is known for its great nymph fishing with Pale Morning Dun nymphs.*

PMDs. As a general rule, I try to fish with the largest tippet possible without jeopardizing strikes. If I'm having difficulty catching plainly visible trout, I switch to a smaller tippet and drop down one hook size.

When hatches are sporadic, I typically drop a Mercury PMD off a caddis larva, Buckskin, or Yellow Sally nymph, which are foods trout are accustomed to eating this time of year. As the hatch intensifies, I switch to two PMD nymphs such as a Mercury PMD with a Bead-Head or Flashback Barr Emerger as the attractor fly. Fishing two Pale Morning Dun nymphs stacks the odds in your favor when the trout are keying heavily on nymphs and emergers. Once the fish commit to the duns, clip off your nymphs and fish dry flies.

## MERCURY TRICO

The next important hatch, especially for small-fly enthusiasts, is the Tricos. From my past experiences, the Trico hatch is less affected by external factors such as bright sunny days or overcast skies, resulting in exceptional dry-fly fishing each day for a several-month period.

Many anglers mistakenly dismiss Trico nymphs, believing that the hatch occurs too early in the morning or late at night to fish. However, I have had amazing results with Trico nymphs at the Dream Stream before the female duns (which have olive abdomens and black thoraxes) started hatching around 7 AM. Trico nymphs are also useful in the evenings when male duns, which are solid black, hatch between 6 PM and dark. In many cases, anglers call it quits and head home before this occurs.

Similar to Pale Morning Duns, Tricos are crawlers and have thick, box-like thoraxes. I tie the Mercury Trico nymph on a Tiemco 101 (as opposed to a 200R) to imitate a Trico's short abdomen and enlarged triangular gills. Trico nymphs vary in color from dark olive to brown depending on the watershed.

### Rigging and Fishing Tips

Most anglers I know fish a Trico nymph like any other mayfly nymph. The only drawback is its size—Trico nymphs are usually a #22 or #24 and tied on a short-shank hook. Hooking a fish on a Trico nymph is not hard, but landing one is a whole different story.

I fish my Trico nymphs dead-drift with a conventional, two-fly nymphing rig. In the morning (6:30 to 7:30 AM), I typically drop a Trico nymph off a flashy midge pattern like a Mercury Midge or Mercury Flashback Black Beauty, since both midges and Tricos are hatching. In the evenings, I drop my Trico nymph off a Buckskin or *Hydropsyche* to match the caddis that hatch in the evening. I tend to concentrate my efforts in shallow, 18- to 24-inch-deep riffles. Like any other mayfly hatch, the aggressive fish will move into prime lies—such as riffles, drop-offs near gravel bars, and mid-channel shelves—to feed.

Once the Trico duns begin hatching, usually enough trout are rising to tempt you to cut off your nymphing rig. In this situation, fish any standard upwing mayfly pattern to imitate the duns. Once the spinners begin to hit the water, I switch to a Stalcup's CDC Comparadun or a Trico spinner pattern.

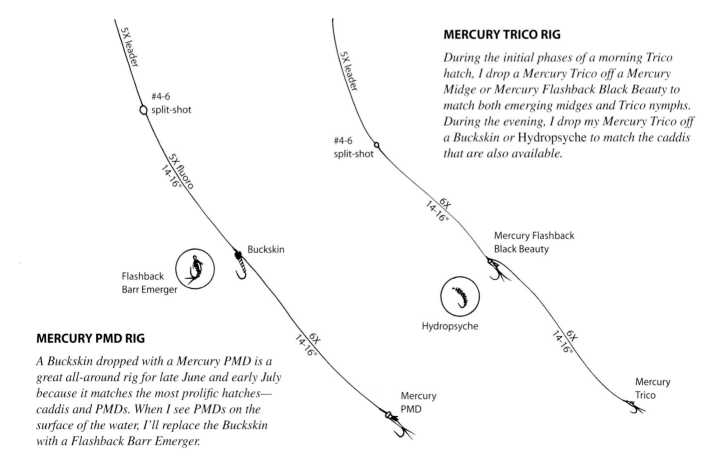

**MERCURY TRICO RIG**

*During the initial phases of a morning Trico hatch, I drop a Mercury Trico off a Mercury Midge or Mercury Flashback Black Beauty to match both emerging midges and Trico nymphs. During the evening, I drop my Mercury Trico off a Buckskin or* Hydropsyche *to match the caddis that are also available.*

**MERCURY PMD RIG**

*A Buckskin dropped with a Mercury PMD is a great all-around rig for late June and early July because it matches the most prolific hatches—caddis and PMDs. When I see PMDs on the surface of the water, I'll replace the Buckskin with a Flashback Barr Emerger.*

## *Mercury Baetis*

| | |
|---|---|
| Hook: | #18-22 Tiemco 200R or #24 Dai-Riki 270 |
| Bead: | Clear, silver-lined glass bead (extra small) |
| Thread: | Light-cahill 8/0 Uni-Thread |
| Tail: | Black saddle hackle fibers |
| Abdomen: | BWO Superfine |
| Wing Case: | Black Z-lon |
| Thorax: | BWO Superfine |
| Legs: | Black Z-lon |

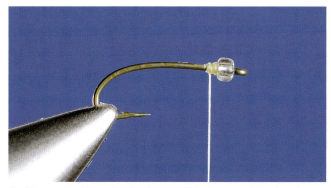

**1.** Place a bead on the hook and slide it toward the hook eye. Insert the hook in the vise, attach the thread behind the bead, and build a thread dam to secure it.

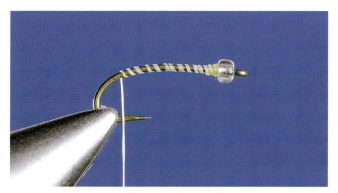

**2.** Wrap the thread back toward the hook bend, stopping at a point on the shank above the barb.

**3.** With your index finger and thumb, stroke the black saddle hackle fibers so that they flare away from the stem.

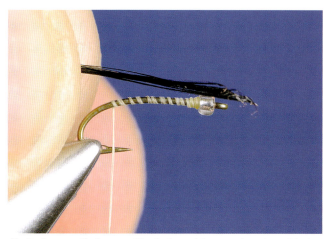

**4.** Grab a small clump of barbules with your thumb and index finger. The tail should be two-thirds the length of the hook shank.

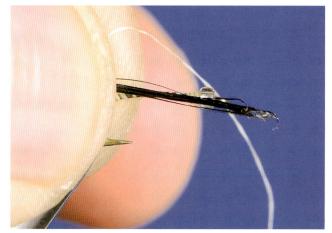

**5.** Grasp the hackle fibers with your index finger and thumb and lay them on the hook shank. Draw the thread back into your thumb and index finger, pinch the thread, and pull the bobbin straight down to secure the tail. Repeat this process twice.

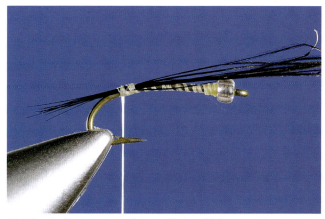

**6.** The tie-in location of the tail should be near the barb. To keep the flare at a minimum, the first wrap should be tight, the second wrap tighter, and the third wrap tightest. The tail should be on top of the shank, with the remaining fibers extending beyond the hook eye.

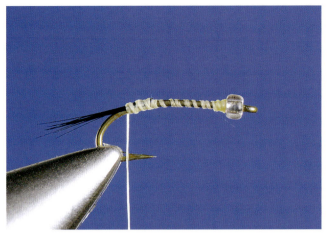

**7.** Clip the butt ends of the hackle fibers and wrap over them with thread. Wrap the thread back to where you tied in the tailing fibers.

**8.** Create a tight dubbing noodle for the abdomen.

**9.** Dub a thin, sparse abdomen two-thirds up the hook shank. The abdomen should be slightly tapered between the tail and thorax.

**10.** Tie in a small clump of black Z-lon for the wing case and tail. Clip the butt ends and bury any remaining exposed Z-lon. The wing case should be just in front of the midpoint on the hook shank.

**11.** Dub the thorax, keeping it thin and sparse. The tie-in point of the Z-lon naturally creates a small taper, so don't get carried away trying to create a taper with the dubbing alone.

**12.** With your thumb and index finger, pull the Z-lon over the top of the thorax and glass bead.

**13.** Secure the Z-lon with two tight wraps of thread. Don't use any more than that to keep the head small.

**14.** Divide the Z-lon clump into two equal parts. Using your thumb and index finger, pull the set of Z-lon legs closest to you back at a 45-degree angle.

**15.** Trap the Z-lon with two tight wraps of thread. Once again, be careful not to create too much bulk around the head.

**16.** Pull the second set of legs back and trap the fibers with two tight wraps of thread.

**17.** Color 6 inches of the thread with a black Sharpie. This should be enough to allow you to make several wraps of thread and a whip-finish.

**18.** Take four to six wraps of thread to finish off the head and cover any of the exposed light-colored thread.

**19.** Whip-finish and trim the thread.

**20.** Trim the legs so that they extend slightly beyond the wing case. Lay your scissors across the hook shank (just behind the wing case) and cut both legs at the same time.

**21.** The tail on the finished fly should be two-thirds the length of the hook shank, and the abdomen should be thin, sparse, and tightly dubbed. The abdomen should be slightly tapered, but do not go overboard. The wing case should extend just short of the legs. Finish the fly with a smooth and symmetrical thread band behind the bead.

### *Mercury Pale Morning Dun*

| | |
|---|---|
| Hook: | #18-22 Tiemco 200R or #24 Dai-Riki 270 |
| Bead: | Clear, silver-lined glass bead (extra small) |
| Thread: | Light-cahill 8/0 Uni-Thread |
| Tail: | Brown saddle hackle fibers |
| Abdomen: | PMD Superfine |
| Wing Case: | Brown Z-lon |
| Thorax: | PMD Superfine |
| Legs: | Brown Z-lon |

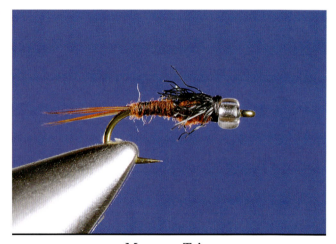

### *Mercury Trico*

| | |
|---|---|
| Hook: | #20-24 Tiemco 101 |
| Bead: | Clear, silver-lined glass bead (extra small) |
| Thread: | Dark-brown 8/0 Uni-Thread |
| Tail: | Black saddle hackle fibers |
| Abdomen: | Rust-brown or black Superfine |
| Wing Case: | Black Z-lon |
| Thorax: | Rust-brown or black Superfine |
| Legs: | Black Z-lon |

# CHAPTER 9

# Tyvek Baetis

Randy Smith's rendition of a tiny, sleek *Baetis* nymph is the ultimate guide fly—easy to tie, realistic, durable, and consistently fools hard-fished trout on just about any tailwater, spring creek, or freestone throughout the United States with moderate to dense populations of *Baetis* nymphs.

In the early 1990s, this was a guide secret at the Blue Quill Angler in Evergreen, Colorado. We fished it hard to the selective Cheesman Canyon trout, and the end result was always a lot of fish regardless of the time of year and hatches. The guide and client success created a ripple effect, and a flow happy of customers rushed into the fly shop to stock their boxes with Smith's pattern, which he simply called the Baetis Nymph. Smith cranked them out by the hundreds of dozens, and yet we still often had empty bins.

Many patterns come and go, but two decades later this fly is still among the guides' favorites because it fools trout consistently under a wide range of conditions. Blue-Winged Olives (*Baetis*) are multi-brooded, with their greatest emergences occurring during the spring and fall. Because of this, several sizes of *Baetis* nymphs remain plentiful in the stream regardless of the season.

During certain times of the day, especially dawn and dusk when the light is low, the nymphs move around the bottom to feed or relocate. Some entomologists call this behavioral drift. Additionally, small flow increases can also dislodge several mayfly nymphs from the substrate, which is called catastrophic drift. It is rare to sample the stomach of a trout with a stomach pump and not find a few *Baetis* nymphs.

*The Tyvek Baetis has been a guide favorite for over 20 years. It fishes well year-round on tailwaters and spring creeks.*
JAY NICHOLS

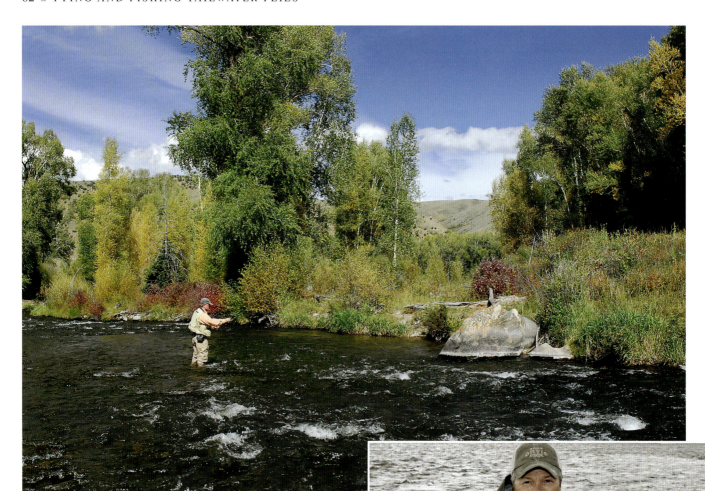

Woody Vogt targets a deep slot on the Williams Fork with a Tyvek Baetis. The Williams Fork is known for its strong autumn Blue-Winged Olive hatches and explosive nymphing each afternoon.

Ron Pecore landed this Madison River brown trout on a Tyvek Baetis.

## RIGGING AND FISHING TIPS

When nothing is hatching, I'll typically dredge this pattern and another nymph under an indicator in the deeper runs and slots. If I'm not tapping the bottom one out of every four drifts, I add more weight until I occasionally pick up moss. My attractor changes with the season. If caddis are present, I'll fish a caddis larva; if Yellow Sallies are present, I'll fish an Oliver Edwards' Yellow Sally nymph, and so on. Midge patterns are also effective year-round.

If I start to see duns, I adjust my weight and target the transitional areas—such as mid-channel shelves and gravel bars—where trout are likely to be suspended mid-column and sweeping back and forth eating huge numbers of Baetis nymphs. Some of the most aggressive feeding patterns occur when trout are feeding on emerging Baetis nymphs. I have watched a trout eat more than twenty swimming Baetis nymphs in one minute.

The trout's feeding behavior will help you decipher whether they are keying on Baetis nymphs. Behavioral clues include a fish lifting in the water column or going out of its way to chase a swimming Baetis nymph. You do not typically see this type of behavior with emerging midges or other types of mayflies.

When the trout become fully engaged on Baetis nymphs, you must have the right size, shape, and color mayfly nymph because they will ignore any other offering. I'll typically fish two Baetis nymphs when this occurs. Other effective patterns include Barr Emergers, Stalcup's Baetis, Mercury Flashback Pheasant Tails, and RS2s. When trout are feeding heavily on Baetis nymphs, you'll need to constantly adjust your weight to get your flies into the correct feeding zone.

## Tyvek Baetis

| | |
|---|---|
| Hook: | #18-24 Tiemco 101 |
| Thread: | Brown 8/0 Uni-Thread |
| Tail: | Wood duck or mallard flank |
| Abdomen: | Olive beaver |
| Wing: | Tyvek colored with black Sharpie |
| Thorax: | Olive beaver |

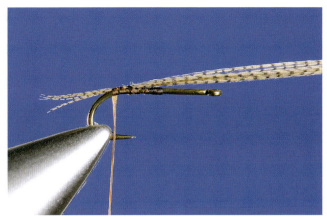

**2.** Wrap the thread back toward a point on the shank above the barb. Strip a few fibers from a mallard flank feather and tie in a tail that is as long as two-thirds of the hook shank.

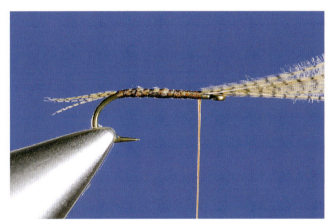

**3.** Wrap the thread forward over the mallard flank, keeping it on top of the hook shank. Strive for a smooth abdomen. Leave the butt ends of the mallard flank extending over the hook eye. They will be used later for legs.

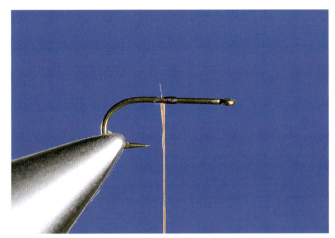

**1.** Place the hook in your vise and attach the thread at the mid-point of the hook shank.

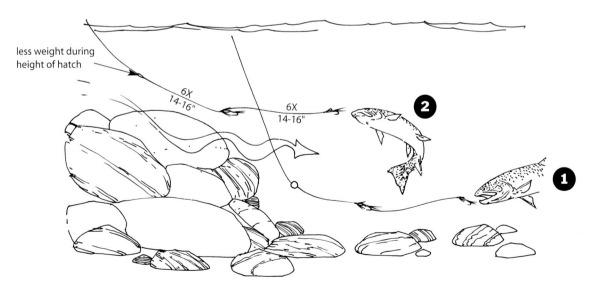

*Baetis nymphs are effective year-round. 1. When there is no evident hatch, fish a Tyvek Baetis with a lot of weight in the deeper slots and runs. 2. During the height of the BWO season (spring and fall), if you begin to see fish flashing, lifting in the water column, chasing mayfly nymphs, or if you see duns on the water, concentrate your efforts in shallow riffles and the transitional zones—mid-channel shelves and gravel bars.*

**4.** Wrap the thread back toward the hook bend.

**5.** Apply a thin layer of dubbing wax to your thread. Make a thin and sparse dubbing noodle with olive-brown rabbit dubbing. With your thumb and index finger, twist the fur onto the thread, applying enough pressure to compact the guard hairs.

**6.** Wrap the dubbing noodle forward to develop a slightly tapered abdomen. Dub the abdomen to the point shown above.

**7.** Using a rotary cutter, straight edge, and self-healing mat, cut a thin strip of Tyvek for the wing case.

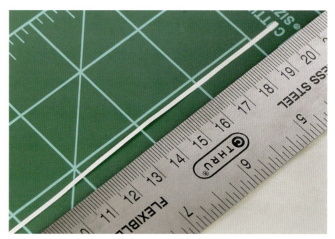

**8.** The Tyvek strip should be equal to about one-third of the hook gap.

**9.** On a piece of cardboard or other scrap material, color the Tyvek strip with a black Sharpie.

**10.** With your material hand, place the Tyvek strip on top of the shank, just behind the hook eye. Make one loose wrap to hold the Tyvek strip in place.

**11.** Make four tight wraps of thread to secure the Tyvek strip. Leave the thread hanging behind the hook eye.

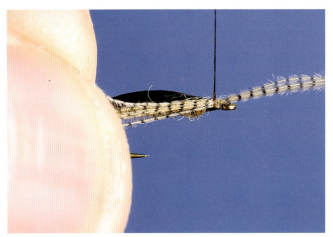

**12.** With your material hand, pull the leg closest to you back at a 45-degree angle and secure it with two tight wraps of thread.

**13.** Repeat the same process with the other leg. Leave the thread hanging in front of the legs.

**14.** Apply a thin layer of dubbing wax to your thread. Make a thin and sparse dubbing noodle with olive-brown rabbit fur. With your thumb and index finger, twist the fur on with enough pressure to compact the guard hairs.

**15.** Finish dubbing the thorax just short of the hook eye. Use only enough dubbing to cover up the wraps of thread used to tie in the wing case and legs. *Baetis* nymphs are thin and sparse. Don't use too much dubbing.

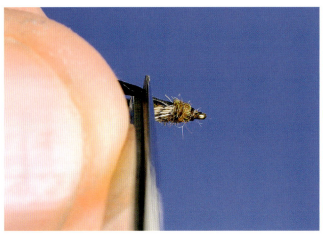

**16.** Trim the legs so that they reach the midpoint. Trim the wing case so that it is approximately 30 percent of the hook shank and just shorter than the legs.

**18.** Top view of the finished fly.

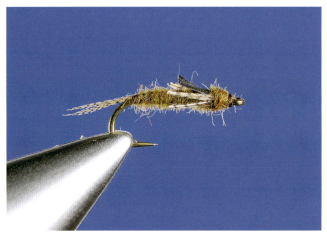

**17.** The finished fly, from the side. The key to a good *Baetis* nymph is keeping a slim profile. Use a small quantity of dubbing and wrap it tightly around the hook shank.

# CHAPTER 10

# *Sparkle Wing RS2*

I have caught more hard-fished, selective trout in Cheesman Canyon with an RS2 than with any other pattern. Over the 20 years that I have been guiding there, the number of fish my clients have caught with it is staggering. The original RS2 was invented by Rim Chung in the early 1970s (RS stands for "Rim's Semblance"). The earlier RS1 had a wing case instead of an emerging wing. Chung's objective for designing the RS2 was to come up with a simple yet realistic nymph that imitated an emerging mayfly. Many variations have spun off the original pattern, including the Sparkle Wing RS2, Mercury RS2, Flashback RS2, and Mercury Flashback RS2.

With no lack of respect toward Chung's original pattern, these offshoots have improved the fly. Many of these variations incorporate synthetic materials, which are easier to find, less expensive, and more durable than the natural materials he used. They are also easier to work with because they are more uniform and consistent. It is much easier to use the same strand of Pearl Braid or Z-lon for a wing rather than stripping webbing off a saddle hackle each time. Superfine dubbing also has no guard hairs, which allows tiers to create thin, tapered abdomens with ease.

All of the variations of the RS2 in this chapter—with different materials, color schemes, flash, and beads—catch fish, but the Sparkle Wing RS2 stands out as my favorite. I'm not alone. It's been a guide favorite at the Blue Quill Angler for over a decade. We have a hard time keeping it in stock, and it

*The Sparkle Wing RS2 is an offshoot of Rim Chung's original pattern. I have fooled trout all over the West with a gray Sparkle Wing RS2.* JAY NICHOLS

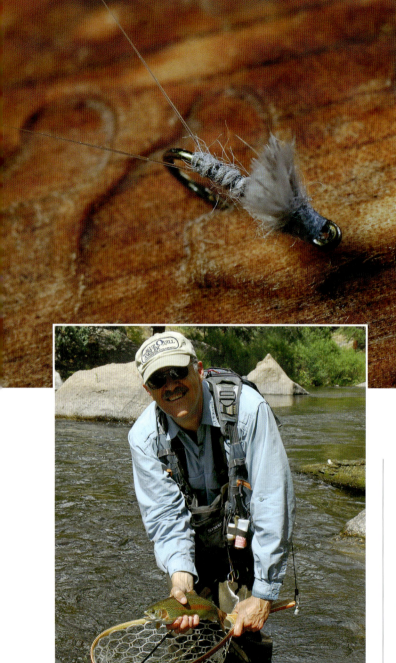

*This is a one of Rim Chung's original RS2s. He sent me two dozen, which I will treasure for a lifetime. Chung's original recipe included a straight-eye hook (Tiemco 101), two moose body fibers for the tail, natural beaver fur, and saddle hackle webbing (the fluffy material near the stem) for the wing. This RS2 tied by Chung uses medium-dun Microfibetts for the tail.* JAY NICHOLS

*The Sparkle Wing RS2 uses a flashy material called Pearl Braid for the emerging wing.*

The Sparkle Wing RS2 was invented by Bob Churchill, who substituted Pearl Braid for the saddle-hackle webbing that Chung used in his original design. Churchill used elk for tailing fibers and did not split them. Instead of elk, I like to use hackle fibers for my tails, but I also do not split them. I have yet to run across a trout that cares whether the tail is split, but do what you feel is best and what you have the most confidence in.

Although the original pattern was gray, you can easily change the color of the dubbing to match just about any mayfly hatch. I also like to use black Superfine on my #24s to imitate midge emergers.

### RIGGING AND FISHING TIPS

I have had great success with RS2s in a variety of conditions, year-round. If the water is high or slightly off-color, I typically fish an RS2 with an attractor like a caddis larva, stonefly, scud, or San Juan Worm. I change the attractor with the season and keep the RS2 as my dropper. In May I might use a caddis larva, in June a stonefly, and if it is the beginning of runoff and the rising flows are knocking loose scuds and aquatic worms, a UV Scud or San Juan Worm. Because mayflies get smaller as the season progresses, in the spring and early summer I use a #18 or #20 RS2; in the fall, a #22 or #24.

When the water is low and clear, I typically drop the RS2 off a midge pattern like a Mercury Midge. On the South Platte River, a #20-22 Mercury Midge dropped with a #20-22 RS2 is especially effective in moderately paced riffles and smooth

*Jim Cannon caught this Cheesman Canyon rainbow with a Sparkle Wing RS2 in the Rainbow Pool.*

is without a doubt one of the best sellers in our shop, which has over 1,400 fly bins.

I believe the effectiveness of this particular variation stems from the emerging wing tied from Pearl Braid, which produces a mirror-like flash as it twists and tumbles in the water. The flash imitates the gases trapped in the thorax area of an emerging *Baetis* nymph as it ascends to the surface of the water. I have watched trout move as far as 18 inches to intercept this fly as it rises in the water column, which gives me the confidence to reach for it often.

slots between the boulders because the flies match midges and mayflies, the most prolific food organisms in the river. Between mid March and May, and then again between late August and early November, I pick up fish on both flies between 9 AM and noon, but as *Baetis* nymphs begin emerging around 12:30 PM, I catch three times as many fish on the RS2 because the trout are keying on mayfly nymphs and emergers. During the height of the hatch, I typically fish the RS2 with another mayfly nymph like a Tyvek Baetis, Mercury Baetis, or a Flashback Mercury Pheasant Tail.

Chung has a unique style of nymphing and sucks trout out of a run as if he was using vacuum cleaner. His rod of choice is a Sage 389 LL with 444 SL running line. He uses a long, tapered leader, formulated to complement his 8-foot, 9-inch, 3-weight. While he does not use a strike indicator, an uncanny ability allows him to feel the strike. He uses a tight-line nymphing technique but allows his flies to swing during the latter part of the drift to imitate emerging mayflies. This unconventional style of nymphing is deadly, drawing many parallels with Czech nymphing. The only difference is that Chung does not use weighted flies; he uses split-shot or moldable putty on his leader to get his flies to the bottom. According to Chung, "The RS2 is an emerger, but it shouldn't be treated as a traditional emerger. It shouldn't be limited to near-surface fishing but rather fished in a classical ascending manner. This fly should be fished as a nymph."

You can also fish this fly as an emerger with the greased-leader technique, which I often do whenever I see head-to-tail rises. To fish this tactic, apply dry-fly floatant to the entire leader except the last 12 inches closest to the fly. The preferred method is to fish your emerger straight upstream. Locating your fly is the greatest challenge when fishing emergers—you need to have a keen eye and set the hook to any rising trout near your flies.

As the hatch intensifies, I switch to two mayfly nymphs or emergers. I typically tie on a #20-22 BWO Barr Emerger,

*The Sparkle Wing RS2 fishes well under a wide range of conditions, but it is most effective during the height of a strong Blue-Winged Olive hatch.* LANDON MAYER

Mercury Pheasant Tail, Tyvek Baetis, or Mercury Baetis as my upper fly, and drop a #20-22 Mercury RS2 or Sparkle Wing RS2 to imitate the emergers, which ride higher in the water column. During the height of the hatch, you'll need considerably less weight than in the beginning, because trout will often chase an emerging *Baetis* 12 to 18 inches as it ascends toward the surface. When the hatch fizzles out, I'll usually switch back to fishing with one midge and one mayfly nymph, in anticipation of the evening midge hatch. If there is a heavy midge hatch, I'll switch my rig to two midge imitations.

I use the same rationale with Pale Morning Dun nymphs, but swap in a PMD Barr Emerger, Mercury PMD, or Mercury Pheasant Tail (sometimes a red Mercury Pheasant Tail) dropped with a PMD RS2. Depending on the flows and water temperatures, trout will begin keying on PMDs as early as mid

*The Sparkle Wing RS2 is an effective mayfly imitation from the bottom to the top. 1. During non-hatch periods, or during the initial phases of a hatch, you can fish the Sparkle Wing RS2 off an attractor like a San Juan Worm on the bottom. 2. As the hatch intensifies, you might fish it mid-column. 3. During the height of the hatch you can fish it on a greased leader in the film.*

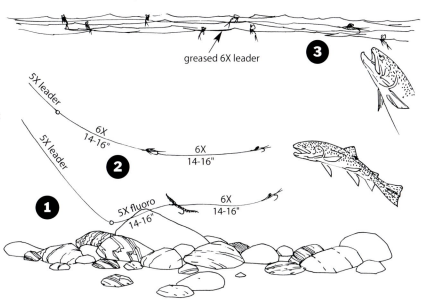

*By changing the color of the dubbing, wing, or adding a bead, you can tweak Rim Chung's original pattern to match any hatch. The Mercury Flashback RS2 can be tied in gray, brown, olive, and black. The most popular sizes are #20 and #22.* JAY NICHOLS

*This Beaverhead brown fell for a #20 gray Mercury Flashback RS2.*

June. You'll need to fish with a #16 or #18 to imitate the nymph. As with *Baetis,* the natural mayfly will become one hook size smaller as the season progresses, so make changes accordingly.

When mayfly hatches have run their course, don't rule out using a small gray or black RS2 to imitate emerging midges. I routinely fish a #22-24 RS2 through the winter because midges are the bulk of a trout's diet between November and March. I typically drop an RS2 off a #22 Rainbow Warrior, Jujubee Midge, Mercury Blood Midge, Mercury Midge, or Black Beauty.

## *Churchill's Sparkle Wing RS2 (Gray)*

| | |
|---|---|
| Hook: | #18-24 Tiemco 101 |
| Thread: | Gray 8/0 Uni-Thread |
| Tail: | Gray elk hair or hackle |
| Abdomen: | Adams gray Superfine |
| Wing: | Pearl Braid |
| Thorax: | Adams gray Superfine |

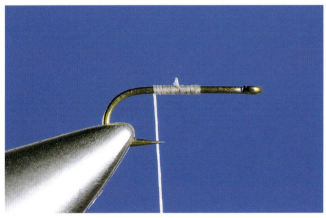

**1.** Place the hook in your vise and attach your thread at the midpoint of the hook shank. Form a smooth thread base, advancing the thread backward one thread width at a time until you reach the place on the shank above the point.

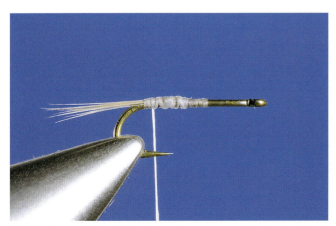

**2.** Tie in spade hackle feathers that are two-thirds of a shank long.

**3.** Dub a thin and sparse abdomen of Superfine. It should have a slight taper from the hook bend to the three-quarter point on the hook shank. Synthetic dubbings allow you to tie a slightly tapered, slender body with ease. The key to a good RS2 is tying it thin and sparse. Natural furs such as beaver have guard hairs, which make them tough to dub and create bodies that look bulkier than the streamlined natural.

**4.** Cut off 6 inches of Pearl Braid to be used for the emerging wing. Pearl Braid is a flat ribbon comprised of several pieces of interwoven Krystal Flash. With your material hand's index finger and thumb, lay the Pearl Braid flat on the hook shank at the point shown above.

**5.** Secure the Pearl Braid with several wraps of thread and smooth out the thread base to prepare for an even thorax.

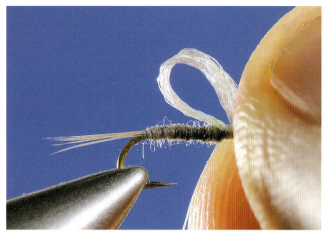

**6.** With your thumb and index finger, form a loop with the Pearl Braid that is about three-quarters the length of the shank.

**7.** Transfer the wing to your left thumb and index finger and pinch it to hold it in place. Make sure the Pearl Braid is flat at the tie-off point.

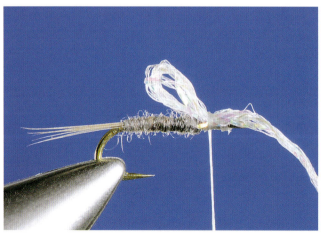

**8.** Make four tight wraps of thread to secure the wing, which should be propped at a 45-degree angle. Leave the thread hanging in front of the wing.

**9.** Clip the extra Pearl Braid. Secure the butt ends and smooth out the thread base. These thread wraps will produce the final taper in the thorax area.

**10.** Dub the thorax from in front of the wing to just short of the hook eye. Make four tight wraps of thread to secure the dubbing.

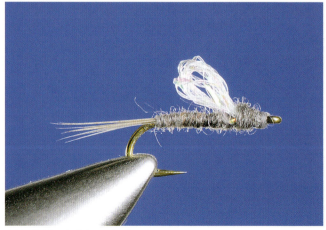

**11.** Whip-finish and clip the thread. The importance of tying this fly thin and sparse cannot be overemphasized. The tail should be two-thirds of a hook shank long, with a slightly tapered abdomen between the tail and the wing. The emerging wing should be pronounced (two-thirds of a hook shank long) and tilted backward at a 45-degree angle.

### Churchill's Sparkle Wing RS2 (Olive)

| | |
|---|---|
| Hook: | #18-24 Tiemco 101 |
| Thread: | Light-cahill 8/0 Uni-Thread |
| Tail: | Natural elk hair or olive hackle |
| Abdomen: | BWO Superfine |
| Wing: | Pearl Braid |
| Thorax: | BWO Superfine |

### Churchill's Sparkle Wing RS2 (Black)

| | |
|---|---|
| Hook: | #18-24 Tiemco 101 |
| Thread: | Black 8/0 Uni-Thread |
| Tail: | Natural elk hair or black hackle |
| Abdomen: | Black Superfine |
| Wing: | Pearl Braid |
| Thorax: | Black Superfine |

### Dorsey's Mercury RS2 (Gray)

| | |
|---|---|
| Hook: | #18-24 Tiemco 101 |
| Bead: | Clear, silver-lined glass bead (extra small) |
| Thread: | Gray 8/0 Uni-Thread |
| Tail: | Gray hackle fibers |
| Abdomen: | Adams gray Superfine |
| Wing: | Glamour Madera (#2400) |
| Thorax: | Adams gray Superfine |

### Dorsey's Mercury RS2 (Black)

| | |
|---|---|
| Hook: | #18-24 Tiemco 101 |
| Bead: | Clear, silver-lined glass bead (extra small) |
| Thread: | Black 8/0 Uni-Thread |
| Tail: | Black hackle fibers |
| Abdomen: | Black Superfine |
| Wing: | Glamour Madera (#2400) |
| Thorax: | Black Superfine |

### Dorsey's Mercury RS2 (Olive)

Hook:       #18-24 Tiemco 101
Bead:       Clear, silver-lined glass bead (extra small)
Thread:     Light-cahill 8/0 Uni-Thread
Tail:       Olive hackle fibers
Abdomen:    BWO Superfine
Wing:       Glamour Madera (#2400)
Thorax:     BWO Superfine

### Dorsey's Mercury Flashback RS2 (Olive)

Hook:       #18-24 Tiemco 101
Bead:       Clear, silver-lined glass bead (extra small)
Thread:     Light-cahill 8/0 Uni-Thread
Tail:       Olive hackle fibers
Abdomen:    BWO Superfine
Back:       Pearl Mylar tinsel
Wing:       Glamour Madera (#2400)
Thorax:     BWO Superfine

### Dorsey's Mercury Flashback RS2 (Gray)

Hook:       #18-24 Tiemco 101
Bead:       Clear, silver-lined glass bead (extra small)
Thread:     Gray 8/0 Uni-Thread
Tail:       Gray hackle fibers
Abdomen:    Gray Superfine
Back:       Pearl Mylar tinsel
Wing:       Glamour Madera (#2400)
Thorax:     Gray Superfine

Note: I tweaked the Flashback RS2 invented by Tom
Whitley, who guides on the Roaring Fork and South Platte
rivers. His variation incorporated a tail of split and clipped
Microfibetts and white ostrich herl for the wing.

### Dorsey's Mercury Flashback RS2 (Black)

Hook:       #18-24 Tiemco 101
Bead:       Clear, silver-lined glass bead (extra small)
Thread:     Black 8/0 Uni-Thread
Tail:       Black hackle fibers
Abdomen:    Black Superfine
Back:       Pearl Mylar tinsel
Wing:       Glamour Madera (#2400)
Thorax:     Black Superfine

# CHAPTER 11

# *Mercury Pheasant Tail*

The Pheasant Tail ranks high among the all-time best trout patterns. Frank Sawyer is credited with designing the original Pheasant Tail back in the early 1930s, which used only pheasant fibers and copper wire, no thread. Sawyer's original concoction had no legs, and the thorax was just wound copper wire. Al Troth's peacock-thorax version with legs is the most common in anglers' fly boxes today.

The Pheasant-Tail Nymph is a generic mayfly nymph that can imitate an assortment of mayflies (#16-22) including Pale Morning Duns, Blue-Winged Olives, Tricos, and Red Quills. For more precise imitations, you can use dyed pheasant-tail feathers—red, black, yellow, olive—to imitate the naturals more closely. For instance, you can use yellow pheasant tail to imitate PMD nymphs or olive ones to imitate *Baetis*.

There have been many variations on the original. You can swap a piece of Mylar tinsel for the wing case (instead of pheasant fibers) for a Flashback Pheasant Tail. The extra flash not only helps the fly stand out, but it also may simulate the flash created by all the tiny bubbles of air on the outer layer of the mayfly nymph's exoskeleton when it hatches. Adding a glass bead also helps impart this illusion.

When I want a pattern that sinks quickly, I use standard brass and tungsten beads, which are heavier than glass beads. My favorite rendition of the Pheasant Tail combines a strip of flash over the back with a gold brass bead, providing the greatest amount versatility and flash. The gold-bead version can be fished in two-fly nymphing rig or used as a dropper off a dry fly. I typically use a tungsten Flashback Pheasant Tail when

*If you fish tailwaters on a regular basis, you'll need a good assortment of Mercury Pheasant Tails.* JAY NICHOLS

*This brown trout took a Mercury Flashback Pheasant Tail during an afternoon Blue-Winged Olive hatch.* JAY NICHOLS

I'm fishing dry-and-dropper rigs because it gets the fly down quicker than a standard brass bead. If I hang up frequently, I switch to a brass bead.

The key to a good Pheasant Tail is tying it thin and sparse. Many tiers use three or four different clumps of pheasant fibers to create the tail, abdomen, wing case, and legs. With this technique, each tie-in and tie-off point creates unnecessary bulk and makes a fairly simple fly more difficult than it needs to be.

Many years ago, Ed Valdez, an accomplished Rocky Mountain tier, showed me how to tie the entire Pheasant Tail with just four pheasant fibers. I stray from this formula slightly and use five fibers for a #16 and three fibers for a #22. After you have completed the wing pad, you'll need to pull out the odd fiber when you pull back the legs to keep them evenly proportioned on each side of the thorax. For example, remove one fiber on a #16 and then pull back two fibers on each side of the thorax to form the legs. This technique includes tying the tail, abdomen, wing case, and legs all from the same clump of fibers, which helps minimize bulk.

It's important to choose the right materials. I typically use long fibers from the center pheasant-tail feather. If the fibers are too short, you will have difficulty tying the fly with the same

group of fibers. Because I like a bushy thorax, I avoid strung peacock herl, which is crammed in a bag and matted down, and use the peacock eyes, which have longer, thicker fibers that create a much fuller thorax that breathes life. From the bottom to the top of the peacock stick (eye), there is a wide range of sizes from #22 to #16, based on the thickness of the herl. You can alter your imitation by tying a thin and sparse thorax, rather than a robust one, to imitate different mayfly nymphs. Pale Morning Duns and Tricos have boxlike thoraxes, whereas *Baetis* nymphs have streamlined thoraxes and abdomens.

### RIGGING AND FISHING TIPS

One of my favorite rigs from June through August is a #18 Mercury Flashback Pheasant Tail dropped off a #18 Buckskin. I routinely fish this rig on the Colorado, Williams Fork, and South Platte to imitate caddis larvae and larger mayfly nymphs such as Pale Morning Duns and Red Quills. Mercury Flashback Pheasant Tails in sizes 20 and 22 fish well year-round because they imitate *Baetis* nymphs. The guidelines and fishing strategies are the same as for the Tyvek Baetis (see page 62). During the spring and autumn, I frequently fish a Mercury Flashback Pheasant Tail as my attractor in a two-fly nymphing rig and drop a small midge larva or pupa below it. If a mayfly hatch is in progress, I'll add another mayfly nymph or emerger such as a Barr Emerger, Sparkle Wing RS2, or Mercury Mayfly.

---

### *Mercury Flashback Pheasant Tail*

| | |
|---|---|
| Hook: | #18-24 Tiemco 101 |
| Bead: | Clear, silver-lined glass bead (extra small) |
| Thread: | Black 8/0 Uni-Thread |
| Tail: | Pheasant-tail fibers |
| Rib: | Fine gold wire, reverse ribbed |
| Abdomen: | Pheasant-tail fibers |
| Thorax: | Peacock herl |
| Wing Case: | Mylar tinsel (small) |
| Legs: | Pheasant-tail fibers |

---

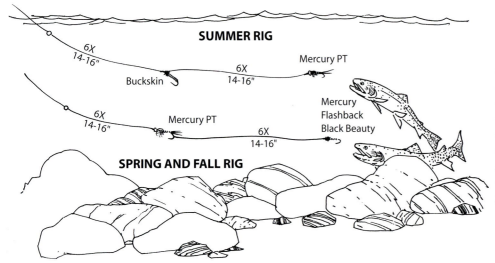

*In a wide range of sizes, the Mercury Flashback Pheasant Tail imitates an assortment of mayfly nymphs, and you can pair it with different flies depending on the season or time of day. I love to fish it behind a Buckskin or drop a Mercury Flashback Black Beauty from it. For sizes 18 and larger, I use 5X fluorocarbon.*

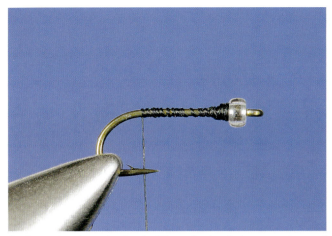

**1.** Put a bead on the hook. Place the hook in your vise and slide the bead behind the hook eye. Attach the thread behind the bead and take several wraps behind the glass bead to hold it in place.

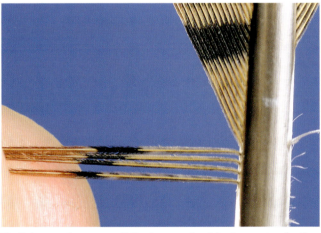

**2.** Select a pheasant-tail feather, preferably the center feather from a pheasant-tail clump. Hold it in your right hand and pull four fibers straight out at a 90-degree angle from the quill. Hold the tips of the fibers to keep them aligned. With your right hand, transfer the material by grabbing the butt end of the fibers.

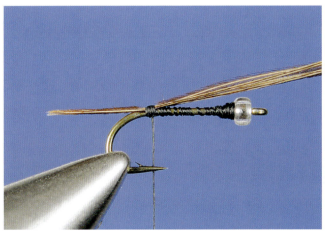

**3.** Lay the four pheasant-tail fibers on top of the hook shank. The tail should be two-thirds the length of the hook shank. Secure the tail with four wraps of thread.

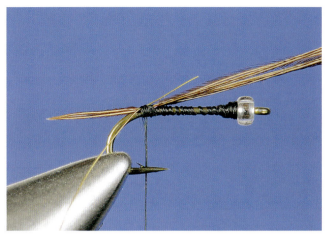

**4.** At the hook bend, lay a piece of gold wire at a 45-degree angle across the hook shank and take two tight turns of thread over it.

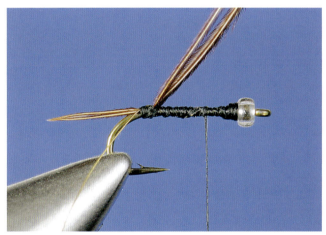

**5.** With your material hand, pull the pheasant-tail fibers back out of the way to expose the gold wire. Wrap the thread forward and around the hook shank, trapping the gold wire. Secure the gold wire in front of the pheasant-tail fibers with three to four tight wraps of thread so that the wire does not come undone when you are wrapping it for the rib. Wrap the thread to the point shown above.

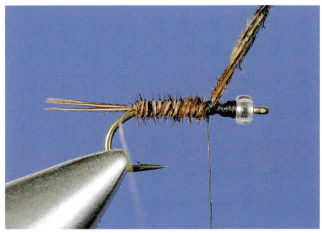

**6.** Wrap the pheasant-tail fibers forward to the point shown and secure them with four tight wraps of thread.

**7.** Wrap the gold wire forward seven times to rib—and reinforce—the abdomen. Tie off the gold wire with four tight wraps of thread.

**8.** Wrap the thread forward, covering the pheasant-tail fibers to the bead. Divide the fibers so that there are two legs on each side of the bead.

**9.** Tie a 6-inch piece of Mylar tinsel in behind the legs and secure it with several wraps of thread. Wrap the thread back to the midpoint on the hook shank, covering the tinsel and pheasant-tail fibers with a smooth thread base.

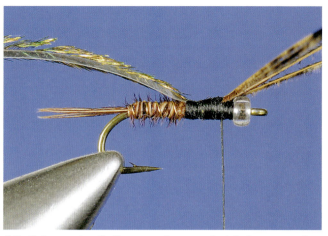

**10.** Select a nice fluffy peacock eye and pick the appropriate size. I tend to like a fluffy thorax, as peacock naturally compresses when it hits the water. I use herl from the peacock eye as opposed to the strung herl, which is often crammed in a bag.

**11.** The size of the peacock herl fibers naturally increases as you progress up the stem. For instance, near the base of the stem the peacock herl is a #22.

**12.** About three-quarters of the way up the stem, you have fibers suitable for #16s.

**13.** Hold a piece of peacock herl in your material hand and clip half an inch off the tip with your scissors. Tie in the herl by the tip at the midpoint on the hook shank and secure it with four tight wraps of thread.

**14.** Wrap the peacock herl forward seven times, ending up just behind the legs.

**15.** Secure the peacock with four wraps of tight thread and clip the butt ends. Leave the thread hanging behind the legs.

**16.** Pull the piece of Mylar tinsel over the top of the thorax and lash it down with two tight wraps of thread.

**17.** With your material hand, pull the leg closest to you back at a 45-degree angle, tie it down, and secure it with two wraps of thread.

**18.** Pull the opposing leg back at a 45-degree angle and secure it with two tight wraps of thread.

**19.** Here is a top view of the legs.

**20.** Whip-finish.

**21.** Trim the legs to length. They should be slightly longer than the Mylar tinsel. Each leg should splay back at a 45-degree angle from the bead. The tail should be two-thirds the length of the hook shank. The abdomen should be thin and sparse with uniform spacing between the segmentation. The wing case should cover 40 percent of the hook shank, with the legs extending slightly beyond it. Finish the fly with a thin, even band of thread behind the bead.

### Mercury Flashback Pheasant Tail (Black)

| | |
|---|---|
| Hook: | #18-24 Tiemco 101 |
| Bead: | Clear, silver-lined glass bead (extra small) |
| Thread: | Black 8/0 Uni-Thread |
| Tail: | Black pheasant-tail fibers |
| Rib: | Fine black wire, reverse ribbed |
| Abdomen: | Black pheasant-tail fibers |
| Thorax: | Peacock herl |
| Wing Case: | Mylar tinsel (small) |
| Legs: | Black Krystal Flash |

### Mercury Flashback Pheasant Tail (Red)

| | |
|---|---|
| Hook: | #18-24 Tiemco 101 |
| Bead: | Clear, silver-lined glass bead (extra small) |
| Thread: | Black 8/0 Uni-Thread |
| Tail: | Red pheasant-tail fibers |
| Rib: | Fine red wire, reverse ribbed |
| Abdomen: | Red pheasant-tail fibers |
| Thorax: | Peacock herl |
| Wing Case: | Mylar tinsel (small) |
| Legs: | Red Krystal Flash |

# CHAPTER 12

# Hi-Viz Mayfly Dun

Mayflies are part of the Ephemeroptera insect order, which literally means "short-lived winged insect." Duns have an opaque upright wing; two or three tails (depending on the species); a sleek, curved body; six delicate legs; and a small pair of hind wings (missing in some species). They quickly undergo a second transformation into sexually mature adults called spinners. Spinners have clear, glasslike wings and form mating swarms before depositing their eggs into the stream. Mayfly duns rarely live longer than 24 to 48 hours because they do not drink any water. The end result is that they dehydrate and perish quickly, unlike caddisflies and stoneflies, which can live for several weeks because they do take in fluids.

Mayflies vary in size from one-eighth inch to over an inch long and come in a wide range of colors, depending on species and habitat. The first mayflies to appear are the Blue-Winged Olives, which start as early as mid March when conditions are right. Ideal conditions include water temperatures reaching the 42 to 44 degree mark with mild, overcast afternoons. Blue-Winged Olive (BWO or *Baetis*) hatches start sporadically, but by the first week of April, anglers will find consistent afternoon hatches from 1 to 3 PM. As the numbers of mayfly duns begin to increase, the trout begin to become aware of their presence. In overcast and inclement weather, you get the best hatches because the duns float on the water for a longer period of time, as their wings take longer to dry. Some of my best days have

*Jim Cannon fishes to a pod of rising fish that are eating Blue-Winged Olive duns in the Jamboree Pool in Cheesman Canyon. A Hi-Viz Mayfly Dun was the perfect candidate to fool these risers. It makes smaller flies easy to see in foam lines, glare, and choppy riffles, and it sits flush in the surface film like the naturals. I tie Hi-Viz patterns in pale olive, sulphur-yellow, olive-brown, mahogany, and black in sizes 16-22 to prepare for just about any hatch of small mayflies.*

*There is nothing more exciting than finding a pod of rising fish that are sipping mayfly duns.* JAY NICHOLS

*Top: Dave Leinweber targets bank sippers feeding on Blue-Winged Olives in Elevenmile Canyon.*

*Some of the best dry-fly fishing occurs on overcast, rainy, or snowy days. Josh Behr shows off a beautiful 20-inch rainbow that he fooled on a cold, blustery winter day.*

been when it snowed or drizzled all day. Under these conditions, scores of rising trout feast on hundreds of mayfly duns. If skies are bright and sunny, mayfly duns dry their wings and leave the water quickly, and the dry-fly fishing is mediocre at best—though fish will still eat plenty of nymphs below the surface.

Pale Morning Duns follow *Baetis,* with their emergences beginning in late June and hatching sporadically through August in many drainages. The best fishing is generally between 10 AM and 1 PM. Once again, expect a full-blown Pale Morning Dun hatch on overcast days. Tricos overlap Pale

*McFlylon is a synthetic material made from polypropylene, which is available in several colors from white to hot pink (cerise). Unlike calf hair, McFlylon is consistently uniform and requires no stacking. The wing size can be altered by removing or adding fibers, and the wing can be trimmed to size with a pair of scissors.* JAY NICHOLS

Morning Duns, and hatch well into autumn. Dun patterns fish well in the evening as the males come off the night before, and then again between 7 and 9 AM. Then the trout switch gears and key heavily on the spinners for a good two hours.

Red Quills begin hatching mid August and last through September, filling an important void between the Pale Morning Duns and Blue-Winged Olives, which begin hatching in September and last sporadically through mid November. If you have difficulty seeing a traditional Catskill-style Red Quill, tie a Hi-Viz variation. I like to substitute dun hackle fibers for the tail, use mahogany synthetic dubbing for the abdomen, and dun hackle for the parachute. Red Quills hatch between 3 and 5 PM and often provide some explosive dry-fly fishing when many anglers have called it quits for the day. You can also tie Hi-Viz variations of other mayfly duns to suit your needs.

## RIGGING AND FISHING TIPS

Once duns start hatching, and I see a fish or two consistently rising, I'll switch to dry flies. When choosing a dun pattern, I often reach for a parachute-style fly that sits flush on the surface film and produces a more lifelike impression. Parachute patterns will fool the most selective trout during a mayfly hatch, especially in glasslike pools where they have plenty of

time to inspect your imposter. For that reason, parachute patterns or Comparadun-style mayfly duns are my go-to patterns to fool trout during a mayfly hatch. Conventional hackled patterns are supported by the tail and hackle, leaving part of the abdomen resting on the surface and the other part slightly above the surface. They are useful when you want to impart a little movement to the fly or fish in heavier currents.

I typically fish my mayfly duns with 9-foot leaders terminating in 6X and 7X tippet. I use 6X for #16 and #18 and 7X for #20 through #24. If you are getting refusals with 6X, drop your tippet size and watch your drag closely. If you notice the fly traveling faster than the current or creating a wake, try moving or changing your angle of attack. Another option is to use a slack-line cast such as an S cast or a reach mend to put a little slack in your line to keep the fly from dragging. In most cases, the fly only needs to float drag-free for a few inches, so don't get carried away trying to create too much slack.

You can fish your Hi-Viz Mayfly Dun a number of ways: upstream, downstream, up and across, or down and across. With an upstream presentation, in theory, you're casting from the trout's blind spot, which reduces the possibility of spooking your target. You will need to be careful, however, not to line your fish with a poorly executed cast. Keep your false casting to a minimum and to the side of your target. From this position, you will pull the fly straight back into the trout's mouth, ensuring a good hook-set.

With a downstream or down-and-across presentation, the first thing the trout sees is the fly, not the fly line or leader, which can put down a rising fish. This position often requires a slack-line cast or mend to offset drag. Be careful with your approach because the trout are facing upstream and are easily spooked by movement or careless wading. Avoid wearing bright clothing and watch the position of the sun so your shadow does not spook any fish. Your greatest challenge with this tactic is getting a good hook-set because you're pulling the fly away from the trout's mouth after it takes. To alleviate this problem, after the trout has taken your fly, allow it to dip its head below the surface of the water before you set the hook.

Another option is an up-and-across delivery. One of the benefits of this approach is that you can cover two to three times the amount of water than the other two previously mentioned methods. With an up-and-across presentation, you'll need to mend your line to offset any drag that occurs from varying cross-stream currents and during the first half of the drift, strip the fly line behind your index finger to control slack, which, if not properly managed, results in poor presentations and hook-sets. Once your flies drift below you, continue mending and feed fly line into the drift to lengthen your presentation. A little bit of slack here is a good thing. In theory, the up-and-across delivery is a combination of the upstream and downstream techniques.

### Hi-Viz Mayfly Dun (BWO)

| | |
|---|---|
| Hook: | #18-24 Tiemco 101 |
| Thread: | Light-cahill 8/0 Uni-Thread |
| Tail: | Medium-dun hackle fibers |
| Body: | BWO Superfine |
| Wing: | Cerise McFlylon |
| Thorax: | BWO Superfine |
| Hackle: | Medium-dun rooster |

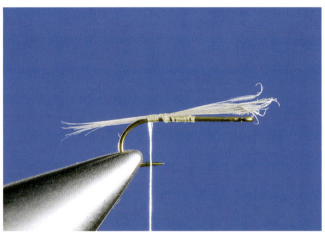

**1.** Place the hook in the vise. Attach the thread with a jam knot at the midpoint of the hook shank. Wrap the thread back to the hook point. Tie in a tail of long, stiff hackle fibers that is the length of the shank.

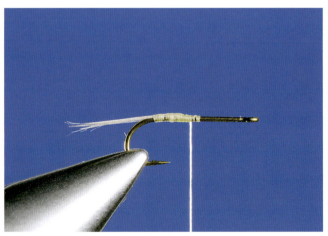

**2.** Clip the butt ends of the hackle fibers and smooth out the thread base.

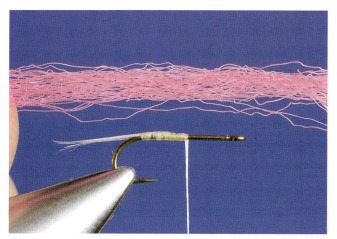

**3.** McFlylon is not as bulky as calf tail or turkey flats at the tie-in point, and I prefer it over spooled Antron, which tends to collapse on the water. (McFlylon holds its shape very well.) Separate one strand from the main bundle. Comb out the fibers with your thumb and index finger to help smooth out some of the kinks. Smooth out the thread base and wrap the thread to the midpoint on the hook shank.

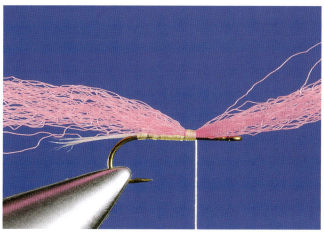

**4.** Lay the McFlylon on top of the hook shank at the point shown above and secure it with six tight wraps of thread.

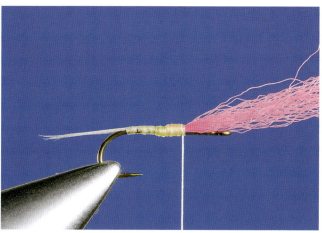

**5.** Clip the butt ends of the McFlylon and smooth out the thread base, leaving the thread at the point shown above.

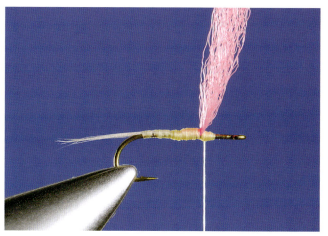

**6.** Prop up the McFlylon with your material hand and wrap a thread wedge in front of the wing.

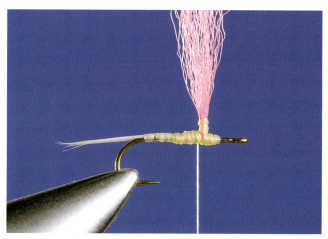

**7.** Start posting the wing by wrapping the thread counter-clockwise around the base of the McFlylon. Start at the bottom of the wing and move up the post one-fifth of a hook shank, one wrap on top of the other, and then retrace your thread wraps and progress down the wing. Secure the post by making one wrap around the hook shank behind the wing.

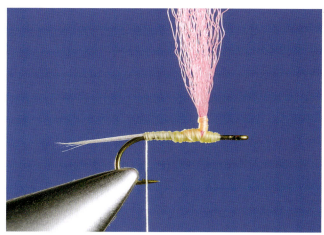

**8.** Smooth out the thread base and wrap the thread back to the hook bend.

**9.** Dub a thin, sparse abdomen with synthetic dubbing. Leave the thread behind the wing.

**10.** Wrap the thread in front of the wing and smooth out the taper between the wing and the hook eye.

**11.** Select a saddle hackle that is 1½ times the width of the hook gap. Strip the barbules from the bottom of the stem. Strip a few additional barbules on the side that will make the first turn against the post.

**12.** Tie the feather with the dull side facing out, in front of the wing, just behind the hook eye, with four tight wraps of thread. The exposed quill should extend slightly behind the wing post.

**13.** Continue wrapping the thread over the stem until you get to the wing post. Wrap the thread around the hackle stem and wing post at the same time from the base to the top. Make these wraps tight and uniform to keep a smooth thread base. Wrap the thread back down the wing post and secure it with a vertical wrap around the hook shank behind the wing. Leave the thread hanging behind the wing.

**14.** Dub the thorax, leaving the thread in front of the wing.

**15.** Starting at the top of the thread post, wrap the hackle down the post in a counter-clockwise motion. Each consecutive wrap of hackle should be directly below the previous wrap. I recommend three to five turns of hackle on a parachute pattern.

**16.** With medium tension, grab your bobbin and hold it at a 45-degree angle behind the hook shank.

**17.** Make a counter-clockwise turn around the base of the wing post and the last turn of the hackle. You want to go in the same direction when tying off the hackle as you did when wrapping the hackle to keep the hackle tight to the wing post. It is important not to trap any hackle fibers with this step.

**18.** Bring the thread up and over the hook shank and wrap the thread behind the eye four times.

**19.** Clip the hackle.

**20.** Whip-finish and clip the thread.

**21.** Clip the wing post so that it is the length of the hook shank (from the base of the wing at the shank to the top of the wing). The tail should also be the length of the shank, and the abdomen thin, sparse, and tightly dubbed. Don't go overboard with the hackle—three or four turns is more than adequate.

### Hi-Viz Mayfly Dun (PMD)

| | |
|---|---|
| Hook: | #16-20 Tiemco 101 |
| Thread: | Light-cahill 8/0 Uni-Thread |
| Tail: | Medium-dun hackle fibers |
| Body: | PMD Superfine |
| Wing: | Cerise McFlylon |
| Thorax: | PMD Superfine |
| Hackle: | Medium-dun rooster |

### Hi-Viz Mayfly Dun (Trico)

| | |
|---|---|
| Hook: | #18-24 Tiemco 101 |
| Thread: | Black 8/0 Uni-Thread |
| Tail: | Medium-dun hackle fibers |
| Body: | Black Superfine |
| Wing: | Cerise McFlylon |
| Thorax: | Black Superfine |
| Hackle: | Medium-dun rooster |

### Hi-Viz Mayfly Dun (Dark Olive)

| | |
|---|---|
| Hook: | #18-24 Tiemco 101 |
| Thread: | Light-cahill 8/0 Uni-Thread |
| Tail: | Medium-dun hackle fibers |
| Body: | Olive Superfine |
| Wing: | Cerise McFlylon |
| Thorax: | Olive Superfine |
| Hackle: | Medium-dun rooster |

# CHAPTER 13

# *Mercury Cased Caddis*

Caddisflies are one of the most widespread aquatic insects, with approximately 1,400 species, outnumbering both mayflies and stoneflies combined. Their abundance is mind-boggling: In many drainages, cased caddis cover the logs, branches, and rocks. On rivers with dense populations of caddis, it is common to impale a cased caddis or two with one of your flies in your nymphing rig. Regardless of the water you fish, chances are good you will encounter moderate to heavy caddis populations. During emergence, the adults produce a blizzardlike hatch with millions of mothlike critters fluttering above the river's surface and buzzing around streamside flora. During a good hatch, the adults crawl up your sleeves, buzz around your face, and get in your glasses.

Caddisflies spend most of their lives as larvae. Most species take about one year to pupate and become adults, but some may complete two generations in a year. Others may require two or three years to reach maturity. Caddis larvae look like grubs, with six prominent legs and tiny hairs covering their abdomens. They are commonly shades of green, olive-brown, and cream, with their heads and thoraxes typically darker than their abdomens.

Caddis larvae fall into one of three categories based on their behavior: free-living, net-spinning, and case-making. Case makers build protective cases out of silt, fine sand, twigs, and other debris. The larvae are completely enclosed within their cases, with the exception of one end, where they stick their

*The Mercury Cased Caddis imitates the* Brachycentrus *caddis, which are easily identified by their brown, rectangular, tapered cases. Inside the casing is a bright-green larva with a dark head, which I imitate with chartreuse Ice Dub and black hare's-mask dubbing. I have found that color drives fish nuts. I'm not sure exactly why, but I don't argue with success.* JAY NICHOLS

The Mercury Cased Caddis is easy to tie and very effective. I carry them in #14-18. The bottoms of many rivers are covered with millions of Brachycentrus caddis, which makes this fly a must. The famous Mother's Day Caddis, which hatches at the end of April and the first two weeks of May, is mostly Brachycentrus. JAY NICHOLS

John Higgs fooled this large rainbow with a Mercury Cased Caddis.

heads out to eat. They attach to logs, branches, and rocks (or wherever they can find protection from predators) with a silk-like material, which they also use to move from one location to another. On many rivers, it's common to pick up a stick, log, or rock that is completely covered with cased caddis.

Trout feed on them by dislodging them from rocks, logs, and aquatic foliage. They also eat them while they are drifting in the current when they lose their footholds and get washed away because of high water (called catastrophic drift), or when they drift in great numbers during certain key periods during the day to migrate (called behavioral drift). Behavioral drift occurs most often during low-light periods (early morning or late in the day), but some case-makers drift midday.

This movement generally occurs when certain areas become overpopulated and the caddis must look for better feeding opportunities. This type of drift provides a steady food source for trout. In *Caddisflies,* Gary LaFontaine notes, "Aquatic insects regulate their feeding areas by the light. Many nymphs and larvae avoid it . . . and during the daytime they remain under stones or vegetation. At night they crawl around on top of bottom objects. A half-hour after dusk and a half-hour before dawn, when they come out in the evening or go in the morning in hasty migration, these insects reach peak rates of behavioral drift."

Some authors, like Mike Lawson and John Barr, talk about heavy concentrations of cased caddis drifting during the middle of the day. Lawson experienced this phenomenon on the Henry's Fork, and John Barr experienced a similar situation on the Colorado River below State Bridge. According to John Barr in *Barr Flies,* "There were thousands of cased caddis drifting downstream just below the surface, and the trout fed on them feverishly."

While you might think that cased caddis are protected, think again. Trout eat the case and all. According to Mike Lawson in *Spring Creeks,* "The protection offered by the case only serves to protect the larvae from other predatory insects. The digestive juices of the trout's stomach quickly digest the larvae and the silks that hold the case together, leaving the remains to be excreted."

Since the Hayman Fire in June 2002, *Brachycentrus* caddis have blanketed the substrate along the South Platte corridor below Cheesman Reservoir and Deckers. Nymph fishermen are constantly removing caddis cases from their flies. Because of their abundant population, they play an important role in the trout's diet clear into the middle part of the summer. Caddis hatches rivaling those on the Arkansas River occur from late May through mid June (later than on freestone rivers). Once Cheesman Reservoir fills up and the excess water flows over the spillway, the water temperatures rise from the warm surface water of the reservoir entering the river. When the temperatures hit the magical mark of 52 to 54 degrees Fahrenheit, adult caddis take to the sky. The Mercury Cased Caddis is also a good pattern on many nearby watersheds like the Eagle, Roaring Fork, Gunnison, and Colorado rivers.

*Since the Hayman Fire in 2002, the caddis populations in Cheesman Canyon have exploded. Anglers will find heavy populations of* Brachycentrus *along the bottom of the river, attached to rocks and twigs. Recently, the Mercury Cased Caddis has become very effective in Cheesman Canyon.*

Trout key on *Brachycentrus* year-round, and they can be especially important foods during the winter. My occasional stomach samples show 14-inch rainbows routinely have a handful of cased caddis in them, even during the dead of winter. Oddly enough, cased caddis often outnumber the midge larvae and pupae in my samples. I believe trout grub cased caddis off branches during the leaner winter months when hatches of midges are the only food organisms available to them.

## RIGGING AND FISHING TIPS

The Mercury Cased Caddis typically fishes best at dawn or dusk when the highest numbers of caddis larvae are drifting in the current. If I notice trout are keying on them (based on pumping the stomach of a fish), I typically fish a Mercury Cased Caddis as an attractor in a two-fly nymphing rig. Also, any time there are flow increases, I consider fishing a Mercury Cased Caddis.

I dead-drift caddis larvae, adding weight until I tap the bottom or collect some moss on one out of every four or five drifts. This ensures the fly is in the right feeding zone, especially for those trout that like to knock loose caddis on the bottom. However, free-drifting caddis may be anywhere in the water column—from just under the surface film to mid-column to rolling along the bottom, so you may need to experiment with weight and where you attach the strike indicator.

### Mercury Cased Caddis

| | |
|---|---|
| Hook: | #16-18 Tiemco 200R |
| Bead: | Clear, silver-lined glass bead (small) |
| Thread: | Tan 8/0 Uni-Thread |
| Abdomen: | Hare's mask and chartreuse Ice Dub |
| Thorax: | Black hare's mask |

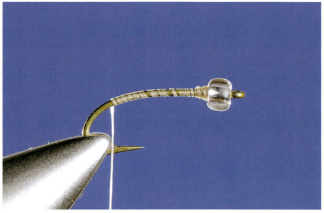

**1.** Place a glass bead on the hook and clamp the hook in your vise. Slide the glass bead toward the hook eye, attach the thread, and wrap a thread dam behind the bead to keep it in place. Wrap the thread back to a point on the shank just above the barb.

**2.** Using a coffee grinder, premix a batch of hare's-mask dubbing with a lot of guard hairs. Apply a thin layer of dubbing wax to your thread, and form a 1½-inch dubbing noodle. Hare's-mask dubbing is harder to work with than synthetic dubbings because of these guard hairs, and you need to twist it more with your thumb and index finger to spin it on the thread.

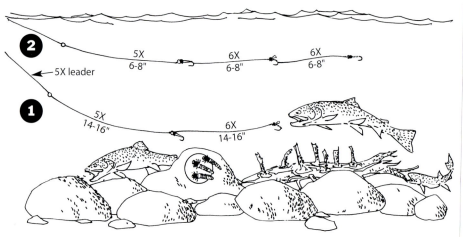

*The Mercury Cased Caddis is a great attractor pattern in a two- or three-fly rig. 1. From November through March, I often connect a #20-24 Top Secret Midge or #20-22 Flashback Black Beauty to the eye of the Mercury Cased Caddis. 2. Because trout generally key on midges this time of year, I'll frequently use a three-fly rig and drop two midges off my Mercury Cased Caddis. From April through September, I typically drop a mayfly nymph, such as a #18-22 red or natural Mercury Pheasant Tail, Mercury Baetis or PMD, or a Sparkle Wing RS2.*

**3.** Wrap the dubbing noodle forward to three-quarters of the way up the hook shank, splaying some guard hairs in the process. Do not clip the guard hairs.

**4.** Wrap the thread back to the point on the shank shown above. Apply another thin layer of dubbing wax to the thread.

**5.** Form another 1½-inch tapered dubbing noodle with the hare's mask. The second layer of dubbing should begin approximately at the barb, which should help you build a slightly tapered abdomen.

**6.** Wrap the dubbing noodle forward over the first layer of dubbing.

**7.** Continue dubbing the abdomen to achieve a nice taper. Pull off any extra dubbing and make four tight wraps of thread to secure it.

**8.** Apply a thin coat of dubbing wax to the thread. Pull some chartreuse Ice Dub out of the package and flatten it out. Ice Dub is coarse and hard to work with, so you will really need to apply pressure with your index finger and thumb when twisting the dubbing noodle.

**9.** Dub a small band of chartreuse Ice Dub equivalent to the thickness of the glass bead. The Ice Dub should be approximately the same diameter as the casing.

**12.** Dub a head that is equal in diameter to the glass bead. Pull the bobbin straight down, exposing 4 to 5 inches of thread.

**10.** Make four tight wraps of thread and leave the thread hanging in front of the chartreuse Ice Dub. Do not worry about any stray pieces of Ice Dub. You will bury them under the head.

**13.** Color the thread with a black Sharpie. Allow the thread to dry for a few seconds before whip-finishing and clipping off the thread.

**11.** Add a thin layer of dubbing wax to the thread. Premix a batch of black hare's-mask dubbing with a coffee grinder. This batch should have fewer guard hairs than the dubbing you used for the casing. Twist a tight dubbing noodle onto your thread.

**14.** The Mercury Caddis should be tapered from the hook bend to the front edge of the casing. Ideally, the dubbing used for the case should have a lot of guard hairs. The protruding larva should have a pronounced head.

# CHAPTER 14

# Bead-Head Breadcrust

The original Breadcrust was developed in northeastern Pennsylvania in the Pocono Mountains by Rudy Sentiwany in the early 1940s. The Breadcrust was popularized by Pennsylvanian Ed Rolka, who tied his first version when he was 13 years old. As a young man, Rolka tied the Breadcrust commercially for fly shops all over the country, including the Orvis Company in Manchester, Vermont. According to Rolka, "The Breadcrust was the hot fly back East!"

In 1970, Rolka moved his family to Denver to accept a job with the Johns Manville Company. Upon his arrival, he sent Bill Logan, outdoor editor for the *Rocky Mountain News,* a few samples of the Breadcrust. Impressed with the fly, Logan wrote a column on it, focusing on two popular fishing destinations—

the Roaring Fork and Frying Pan Rivers—which were known for their dense caddis populations.

"After the article, I sold 20 dozen Breadcrusts to Ken Walters down at The Flyfisher Ltd. in Cherry Creek. Walters had to reorder the next day because they were all gone," said Rolka. Word spread quickly, and soon fly shops all over the central Rocky Mountain region filled their bins with Breadcrusts.

In the mid-1990s Rolka retired from tying the Breadcrust and let me carry on his legacy. I was honored to keep his tradition alive, and he showed me his trade secrets to tying the pattern. Without a doubt, the preparation of the materials is the most difficult part of the fly. Rolka showed me how to trim the barbules, soak and split the quills with a double-edge razor

*The Breadcrust is one of the most versatile caddis patterns ever fished. In two different color schemes—red (reddish brown) and olive—it can imitate free-living caddis, net-spinners, and cased caddis. I carry it in sizes 10 through 18, in both colors, with and without beads. Over the years, a #16 red Breadcrust has been my best producer.* JAY NICHOLS

Forrest Dorsey nymphs with a Bead-Head Breadcrust during the latter part of May. Over the years, the Bead-Head Breadcrust has become one of his favorite flies.

This is one of Ed Rolka's Breadcrusts. JAY NICHOLS

This Blue River rainbow took a Bead-Head Breadcrust. The Blue has a robust population of caddis larvae, especially below Green Mountain Reservoir. The brass bead simulates the prominent gas bubble on emerging caddis pupae.

blade, and clean the pith from the center of the quill. Once the materials were prepared, tying the fly was fairly easy. I quickly learned the importance of preparing a batch of tails at a time to speed up production. Within a month, I began filling Breadcrust orders for 20-plus fly shops throughout the Rockies. I later developed the Bead-Head Breadcrust (tungsten and brass) as well as an olive version.

Finding a red-phase ruffed-grouse tail in the West is no easy task, and Rolka supplied most of the fly shops in Denver with red-phase grouse tails because there was no reliable outlet from which to purchase them. When he retired, Rolka gave me a list of hunters that had been supplying him with grouse tails for many years. Once I got a surplus, I also sold grouse tails to Denver fly shops.

## RIGGING AND FISHING TIPS

April and May are two good months to fish a two-fly rig consisting of a Bead-Head Breadcrust and a Sparkle Wing RS2 or a Mercury Pheasant Tail. This rig covers caddis and *Baetis,* two of the most prevalent food organisms at that time of the year. I typically fish these patterns dead-drift, but let the flies swing during the last quarter of the drift. As the leader tightens on the swing, the Bead-Head Breadcrust rises in the water column like an emerging caddis pupa. This swinging action is also an important tactic with conventional nymphing rigs. You can also fish a Bead-Head Breadcrust down and across like a conventional wet fly, letting it swing gently into the trout's feeding lane. I always recommend setting the hook before recasting your flies to see if a trout may have taken your fly on the rise.

Another effective strategy is to fish your Bead-Head Breadcrust under a buoyant dry fly such as a Puterbaugh Caddis, Elk-Hair Caddis, or Goddard Caddis. Caddis pupae often drift long distances in the water column before emerging into adults, making this tactic extremely effective. Once again, allow your fly to swing in the current to entice fish into striking. You may also skate or skitter your fly to trigger a strike on either the adult or the pupa.

**2.** The underbody is constructed from a four-strand knitting yarn. Divide the four-strand yarn into two pieces.

## Bead-Head Breadcrust

| | |
|---|---|
| Hook: | #12-18 Tiemco 5262 |
| Bead: | Brass ($\frac{1}{8}$" or $\frac{3}{32}$") |
| Thread: | Brown 6/0 or 8/0 Uni-Thread |
| Abdomen: | Red-phase ruffed-grouse quill |
| Underbody: | Black yarn |
| Collar: | Grizzly hen |

**3.** Fasten two strands of yarn behind the bead. Let the thread hang down; you will use it to tie off the underbody.

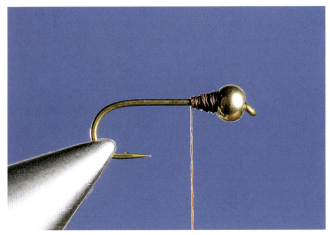

**1.** Place a brass bead on your hook with the small opening near the eye. Put the hook in your vise. Attach the thread behind the bead and wrap a thread wedge to secure the bead.

*I typically fish a Breadcrust as the upper fly and connect a #18-20 Sparkle Wing RS2 or Flashback Mercury Pheasant to the eye with 14 to 16 inches of tippet. At the end of the drift, let the fly swing up in the water column.*

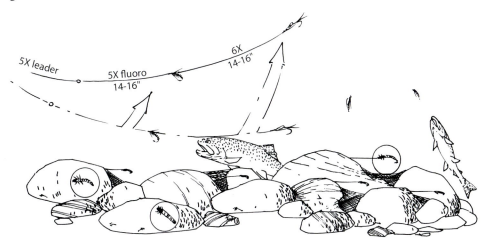

**4.** Wrap the two strands of yarn back toward the hook bend. Keep the wraps symmetrical and tight.

**5.** Wrap the two strands of yarn forward and tie them off. Leave a thread band equal to the width of the brass bead to avoid crowding the thorax area.

**6.** Secure the yarn and clip any excess. Make four tight turns of thread to bury the tag ends.

**7.** Wrap the thread back to the hook bend. As you progress toward the hook bend, make each wrap consecutively tighter to produce a slight taper in the abdomen.

**8.** Select a grouse feather from the tail clump. On average, there are 18 feathers per clump, and you can tie more than two dozen flies with each clump.

**9.** With your left index finger and thumb, grab the grouse feather and clip off the top part. I typically cut off about an inch.

**10.** Flip the feather over and clip the butt end just beyond the webbed part of the feather.

**11.** Holding the grouse feather in your left hand, trim the barbules close to the center quill. The barbules should extend a little less than 1/16 inch from the center quill.

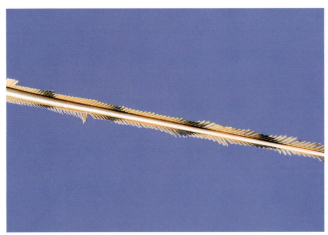

**12.** Repeat the same process on the other side of the quill.

**13.** In a long dish, soak the quill in water for at least 10 minutes. The longer you soak the quills, the more pliable they become.

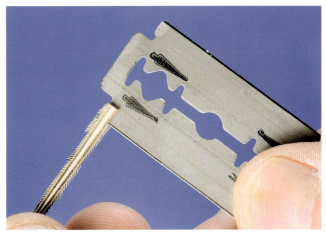

**14.** Split the quill in half with a double-edge stainless-steel razor blade. The razor blade should run parallel to the barbules on the center quill.

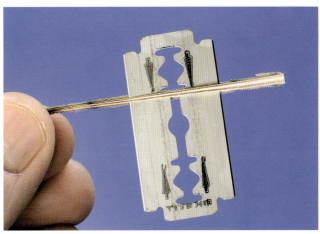

**15.** Carefully guide the razor blade behind the barbules. This will take some practice to become proficient. You may ruin a few feathers attempting this procedure. Don't get discouraged—keep practicing.

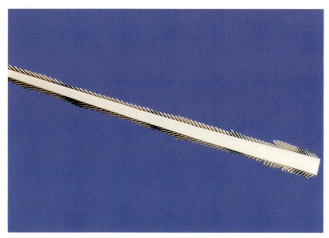

**16.** Discard the bottom part of the quill. If you flip the quill over, you'll notice there is pith inside it.

**17.** Place the quill on a dampened cutting board. Scrape the pith out of the feather with a single-edge razor blade. Take extreme care not to rip off any of the barbules during this process.

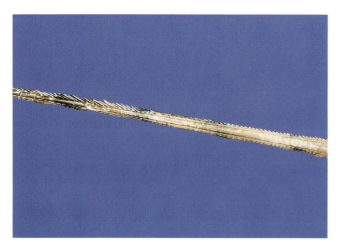

**18.** When the pith is removed, the quill becomes very flexible and easy to use. Place the quill back into the water.

**19.** Grab a quill out of the water dish and tie it in by the tip with four tight wraps.

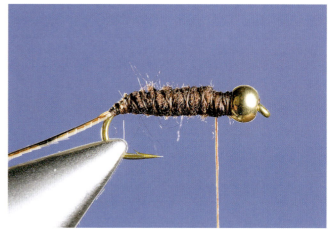

**20.** Tie the quill down slightly beyond the underbody to establish a taper at the rear of the abdomen. Wrap the thread forward to the thread band behind the bead.

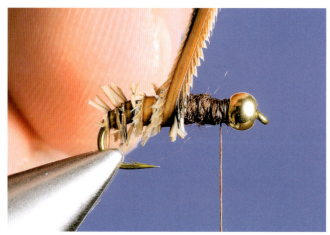

**21.** With your thumb and index finger, wrap the quill forward (clockwise), making sure the wraps are right next to each other. As you wrap the quill forward, the barbules flare, producing a segmented abdomen.

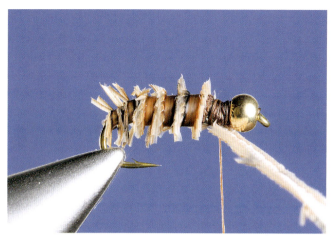

**22.** Stop wrapping the quill when you get to the thread band. Tie off the quill and secure it with four wraps of thread.

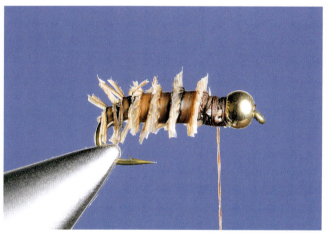

**23.** Clip the quill and secure the butt end with four more wraps of thread. The diameter of the thread band should be slightly less than that of the abdomen. Be careful not to create too much bulk in this area.

**24.** Size and tie in a grizzly hen hackle. The hackle will be wrapped as a collar that sweeps back.

**25.** Wrap the hackle forward, taking three to four turns. Tie off and secure it with four wraps of thread. Clip the excess hackle as close as you can to the thread band.

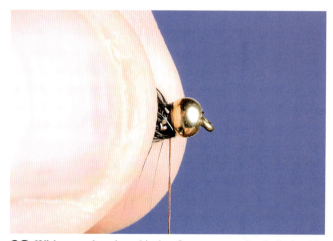

**26.** With your thumb and index finger, sweep back the hackle and make four to six wraps to trap the hackle in place. You may need an additional wrap or two to pull back any stray hackle fibers.

**27.** Make sure your thread collar is smooth and even. Whip-finish and clip the thread.

**28.** Apply a few drops of thin head cement, allowing it to penetrate into the hackle to hold it in place. Thin head cement will not have any negative effects on the hackle.

**29.** A correctly tied Breadcrust should have a slightly tapered abdomen and a collar that gently sweeps back, with a few barbules extending slightly beyond the hook point. Make sure the bead is straight and finished off with a small, clean thread collar.

### Bead-Head Breadcrust (Olive)

| | |
|---|---|
| Hook: | #12-18 Tiemco 5262 |
| Bead: | Black-colored brass bead ($1/8$" or $3/32$") |
| Thread: | Brown 6/0 or 8/0 Uni-Thread |
| Abdomen: | Gray-phase ruffed-grouse quill dyed olive |
| Underbody: | Black yarn |
| Collar: | Grizzly hen dyed olive |

### Breadcrust

| | |
|---|---|
| Hook: | #12-18 Tiemco 5262 |
| Thread: | Black 6/0 or 8/0 Uni-Thread |
| Abdomen: | Red-phase ruffed-grouse quill |
| Underbody: | Black yarn |
| Collar: | Grizzly hen |

# CHAPTER 15

# *Hydropsyche*

Spotted Sedge (*Hydropsyche*) larvae range in size from ¼ to ¾ inch long. They are green to brown in color and thrive on clean substrates with medium- to fast-paced flows. According to Rick Hafele in *Nymph Fishing Rivers and Streams*, "If there is one group of caddisflies you should know and be prepared to imitate, it is the net-spinning caddis."

Net-spinning caddis larvae look similar to the green rockworm, or *Rhyacophila*. Since they have a similar color, the same shape abdomen, and they thrive in comparable habitats, this generic caddis larva imitates both varieties. Hafele also mentions that the populations of net-spinning caddis are typically higher in tailwater fisheries because zooplankton and phytoplankton are washed downstream from the base of the dam, providing an excellent feeding opportunity for the larvae.

My fishing buddy Harold Tygart developed this fly back in the mid-1980s to imitate caddis larvae in the South Platte River near Deckers. The South Platte has always been known for its small aquatic life, especially small midges and mayflies. The river had sporadic hatches of caddis, but since the Hayman Fire in 2002, populations have boomed and now rival those on the Arkansas River.

Before the fire, it was hard to go wrong with a tan San Juan Worm or an orange scud with a RS2 dropper from May through September. Fluctuating flows from the base of Cheesman Dam

*I learned how to tie the Hydropsyche 25 years ago from my fishing buddy Harold Tygart. It is easy to tie, very durable, and catches fish on a regular basis. This is the ultimate guide fly during the spring and summer, and it has become my secret weapon in Cheesman Canyon.* JAY NICHOLS

*The Hydropsyche (middle row) is an olive-brown grublike caddis larva that imitates the net-spinning caddis. This imitation is extremely important for tailwater anglers.* JAY NICHOLS

# SHORT-LINE NYMPHING

As the name implies, the main emphasis with short-line nymphing (also called high-stick nymphing) is using a small amount of fly line. To do so, you must get as close to the fish as possible without spooking them. This enables you to minimize the amount of fly line on the water, which eliminates the need to mend. Because your line is tight to the fly, you can set the hook efficiently with a quick lift of the rod tip. This method is effective in riffles, runs, slots, 6- to 10-foot-wide gravel bars and mid-channel shelves, and pocketwater where repeated casting is mandatory for success.

My typical short-line nymphing rig consists of a 7½-foot tapered leader terminating in 5X or 6X tippet. Using a shorter leader keeps the overall length of the rig as short as possible. I attach an additional 14 to 16 inches of 5X or 6X tippet to the end of the tapered leader with a blood or surgeon's knot to prolong the life of the leader. If you tie your upper fly on the end of your leader, you'll quickly destroy its original taper as you change flies. After you change or replace several flies, you will need to add a new piece of tippet.

To complete my rig, I attach a yarn strike indicator at 1½ to 2 times the depth of the water from the weight and a piece of split-shot or tungsten putty, or a combination of both, 14 to 16 inches above my upper fly. In short-line nymphing, the strike indicator does most of the fishing for you. When properly adjusted, it suspends your nymphs in the water column and keeps them from snagging the river bottom.

I begin by roll-casting no more than 6 to 8 feet of fly line upstream at a 45-degree angle into the oncoming current. Once my flies hit the water, I immediately lift all the fly line and the butt end of my leader above my strike indicator off the water. Longer 9- and 10-foot rods allow you to reach farther across the current. If your strike indicator turns upside down, you are holding too much line off the water and you should give your line a few inches of slack.

Impeccable line management is one of the key ingredients for success. As your flies float down the river, keep your elbow high, your arm parallel with the water's surface, and your rod tip pointed at the strike indicator. As your flies get downstream of you (about 45 degrees), slowly lower your rod tip to extend your drift.

Throughout the drift, strike if your indicator slows down, twitches sideways, or sinks. It is okay to have an inch or two of slack near the leader butt, but any line on the water results in drag. To manage your line, place your line under your casting hand's index finger and strip in slack fly line behind your index finger with your opposite hand.

While your strike indicator can provide clues to a take, you should not rely solely on it. Slack between your strike indicator and flies can delay the detection of the strike. In addition to watching your indicator, also look for any movement, mirrorlike flashes, or fish opening their mouths (noticeable white spots the size of a ping-pong ball) below your strike indicator.

When you do set the hook, make it firm, but use a limited range of motion—12 to 18 inches—to prevent broken tippets. Set straight up in the air or downriver to ensure the hook sinks into the trout's jaw. If you set the hook upriver, you're either pulling the flies out of the fish's mouth or embedding the hook poorly, causing it to slip when you are fighting the fish.

Once my flies have finished swinging in the current, I set the hook, whether or not I detect a take. During certain hatches (caddis and Blue-Winged Olives, for instance) letting your fly swing in the current will often entice a strike, and if you set the hook religiously after each drift, you'll be amazed at how many fish you catch that you never realized were taking your fly.

*Short-line nymphing is my preferred tactic for fishing tricky currents or to fish that I can spot. You must keep the fly line off the water and manage slack line carefully.*
JAY NICHOLS

*Kayle Wilhelm fishes a Hydropsyche in the Mini Canyon above the hamlet of Deckers. The Hydropsyche has become one of my favorite attractors in my two-fly rigs when I fish Deckers and Cheesman.*

constantly knocked loose scuds, crane flies, and aquatic worms, often making the trout gluttonous. It was common to see aquatic worms dangling out of a trout's mouth several hours after a release from the base of Cheesman Dam.

Since the fire, populations of aquatic worms and scuds have diminished because all the decomposed granite that entered the river ruined their habitat. But the caddis numbers are way up. My summer rig on the South Platte River is now a caddis larva and a mayfly nymph (Sparkle Wing RS2, Mercury Flashback RS2, or Mercury Flashback Pheasant Tail) or midge pattern (Top Secret Midge or Mercury Midge). Opportunistic trout are always looking for bigger bites such as caddis larvae, but these are especially effective during a flow increase, when the insects are swept away.

### RIGGING AND FISHING TIPS

Free-living and net-spinning caddis favor oxygenated water, so I tend to concentrate my efforts while fishing this fly in pocketwater and faster riffles and runs. I generally dead-drift it along the bottom with another fly, usually a mayfly emerger. I have watched trout move as far as 18 inches to eat this fly on the first drift.

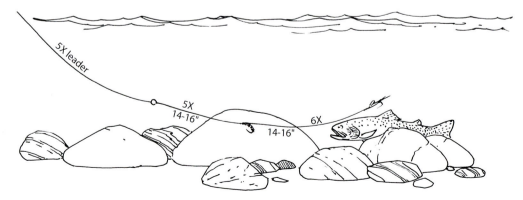

*I use a 7½-foot tapered leader that terminates in 4X or 5X. I typically fish the Hydropsyche as an attractor and tie another mayfly nymph, such as a Mercury Flashback RS2, Barr Emerger, or Mercury Pheasant Tail, to the eye.*

### *Hydropsyche*

Hook: #14-18 Tiemco 2457
Thread: Black 6/0 Uni-Thread
Anal Claws: Peacock Wapsi Life Cycle dubbing
Abdomen: Olive-brown Wapsi Life Cycle dubbing blend
Head: Peacock Wapsi Life Cycle dubbing
Rib: Brown D Rib

Note: For the abdomen, mix 60 percent light-olive Wapsi Life Cycle with 40 percent brown caddis in a coffee grinder.

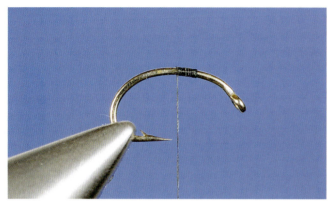

**1.** Place the hook in the vise and attach the thread at the midpoint.

**2.** The abdomen has two different colors of dubbing—a dark olive for the anal and head area and an olive-brown for the abdomen.

**3.** Wrap the thread backward to the hook bend, creating a uniform thread base. Leave the thread at a point on the shank just behind the barb.

**4.** Wrap a small ball of dubbing to imitate the anal claws. Leave the thread slightly in front of the barb.

**5.** Tie in a piece of brown D Rib just in front of the anal claws. Make sure the flat side faces down on the hook shank. Use medium for #14 and small for #16-18.

**6.** Dub the abdomen with the olive-brown mix, leaving enough room for the head, which should be the same width as the anal claws.

**7.** Wrap the D Rib forward clockwise four to five times to create segmentation. The spacing between each wrap should be equivalent to the width of the D Rib. With four tight wraps of thread, tie off the D Rib and clip the butt end.

**8.** Dub the head area so that it is the same width as the anal claws. Secure the dubbing with four tight wraps of thread behind the hook eye.

**9.** Whip-finish, clip the thread, and apply two drops of a thin cement to the head. I use Doug's Head Cement.

**10.** The Hydropsyche should look like a grub. It should have a pronounced anal claw and head that are considerably darker than the rest of the abdomen. The dubbing should be even throughout, with noticeable segments between the anal claws and head.

### Bead-Head Hydropsyche

| | |
|---|---|
| Hook: | #14-18 Tiemco 2457 |
| Bead: | Black tungsten (⅛" and ³⁄₃₂") |
| Thread: | Black 6/0 Uni-Thread |
| Anal Claws: | Peacock Wapsi Life Cycle dubbing |
| Abdomen: | Olive-brown Wapsi Life Cycle blend |
| Head: | Peacock Wapsi Life Cycle dubbing |
| Rib: | Brown D Rib |

Note: For the abdomen, mix 60 percent light-olive Wapsi Life Cycle with 40 percent brown caddis in a coffee grinder.

# CHAPTER 16

# *Buckskin*

The Buckskin was invented in 1972 by veteran South Platte angler Ed Marsh of Colorado Springs. In the beginning, it was constructed from a thinly sliced piece of orangish buckskin. The buckskin strip was slightly tapered and tied in with the rough side out, which created a segmented body as the material was wrapped around the hook.

Marsh's original Buckskin had a small tail and swept-back beard tied from brown hen hackle that simulated legs. Bob Saile, a good buddy of mine, and former outdoor editor for the *Denver Post,* had a similar version he called the Chamois Skin. It also had a hackle beard similar to the original Buckskin, but it had no tail. It was one of Saile's favorite flies on the South Platte near Deckers and Trumbull.

Today's version is a combination of these two patterns. Since buckskin is thick and awkward to work with, especially when trying to construct a thin abdomen, most tiers today use a new car chamois. Some also use Hareline's Micro Tubing (Buckskin), which also alleviates the problem of creating too much bulk.

If you use a car chamois, which you can purchase from just about any outlet that sells auto supplies, look for one that is thin and smooth on both sides. Chamois that is rough and fuzzy

*My friends and I have fooled trout all over the West with Buckskins. Dr. Bob "Hawkeye" Randall fishes a glassy pool with a Buckskin dropped with a Sparkle Wing RS2. This rig has proven itself over the years to be a real winner.*

*I keep my tailwater box stocked with a bunch of #16-20 Buckskins—a #18 is my favorite.* JAY NICHOLS

*The Buckskin is an excellent imitation for a caddis larva. This brown trout was fooled with a Buckskin on the Colorado River below the confluence of the Williams Fork.* JAY NICHOLS

will fall apart and won't produce a thin abdomen. Spend a few extra bucks on a high quality chamois to prevent frustration down the road.

A chamois has a distinct grain. If you stretch it, it will have considerably more resistance to stretching against the grain. After you find the direction of the grain, mark an arrow on the top right corner of the chamois with a Sharpie to indicate its direction.

Next, slice the chamois with a razor blade or rotary cutter on a cutting board or self-healing cutting mat. You want to slice the chamois as thin as possible without having the material break when you wind it around the hook. The strips should be about one half of a hook gap wide. If you cut your strips with the grain, the chamois will fall apart. Cut it against the grain and it will be strong. Another trick is to tie in the chamois along the hook shank and spin it with your index finger and thumb before wrapping it around the hook shank. This will almost guarantee that the chamois strip will not break, plus it gives the abdomen a nice, segmented look.

Most tiers use brown hen-hackle fibers for a tail, keeping the tail about two-thirds the length of the shank. Some tiers use black thread for the head; others use peacock herl. On the standard Buckskin, for ease and simplicity, I use black thread. After you put a couple of drops of cement on the bead, it is bombproof. On the bead-head, I eliminate the tail to make the fly even easier to tie.

## RIGGING AND FISHING TIPS

Don't let the simplicity of the Buckskin fool you. I have caught countless brown trout with this pattern, especially on rivers like the South Platte, Colorado, Williams Fork, Blue, Eagle, Gunnison, and Roaring Fork. The Buckskin fishes well anywhere there are free-living caddis. In smaller sizes, it also looks like a midge larva.

I most often fish the Buckskin as an attractor, or upper fly, in a tandem rig, dredging it along the bottom of a stream where you would typically expect to find caddis larvae. It is very effective in moderately paced riffles and runs as well as pocketwater.

# LONG-LINE NYMPHING

Long-line nymphing allows you to double or triple the amount of water you can cover with a single drift. Also, in some situations you must cast a good deal of line to reach prime lies. This is common on some of the larger Western tailwaters like the Bighorn, Madison, North Platte, San Juan, Green, and the Colorado at Lee's Ferry, where anglers need to target huge gravel bars in the middle of the river. When the best structure is where you cannot safely wade, you either have to fish it from a boat or use long-line nymphing.

Begin by making a long cast 45 degrees upstream and follow it with a large roll-cast mend to stack fly line above the strike indicator. Continue throwing mends into your fly line as your nymphing rig floats downriver. To extend the drift, feed slack into your line as the indicator floats past you. By introducing slack into the second half of the drift, you can theoretically fish your entire fly line, though setting the hook becomes problematic as you increase the distance between you and your flies.

Casting a nymph rig with two or three flies, weight, and a strike indicator can be difficult. Slow down your cast to create a wider loop and prevent tangles. Avoid stopping the rod tip abruptly on the forward stroke (like you would when fishing with dry flies); otherwise you'll get a bird's nest. Keep the slack in the fly line managed to increase your odds of a good hook-set, and strike more aggressively if you have a lot of line on the water.

**1.** I like to use a roll-cast mend to stack the fly line above my strike indicator to compensate for drag. After your cast, bring the rod back toward your chest, creating some slack in the fly line. Accelerate the rod tip forward to shoot fly line upstream.

**2.** Keep the rod tip high, allowing the fly line to unfold as it progresses upstream.

**3.** The weight of the fly line will carry it above the strike indicator.

**4.** Completed roll-cast mend. Repeat as necessary to keep the fly line above the indicator.

## Buckskin

| Hook: | #16-20 Tiemco 100 |
|---|---|
| Thread: | Black 8/0 Uni-Thread |
| Tail: | Brown hen hackle |
| Body: | Thin chamois strip |

**3.** Clip the butt ends of the hackle and secure with four wraps of thread. Wrap the thread forward, producing a smooth and symmetrical thread underbody.

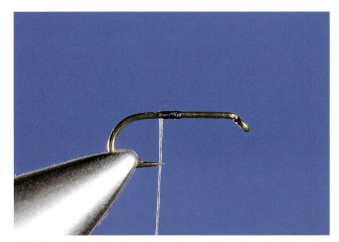

**1.** Place the hook in the vise and attach the thread at the point shown above.

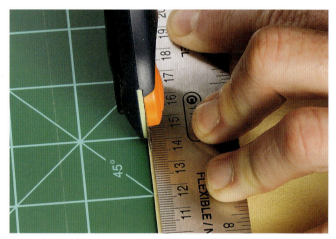

**4.** Use a self-healing mat, rotary cutter, and straight edge to trim your chamois strip. Make sure you are cutting against the grain to increase the strength of your chamois strip. If you cut with the grain, your chamois strip will fall apart.

**2.** Tie in a tail from brown hen hackle. The tail should extend two-thirds of the shank.

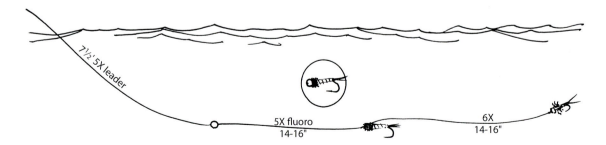

*Between May and August I typically fish my Buckskins (#16-20) with a #18 Flashback Barr Emerger (PMD), Mercury PMD, or a Mercury Flashback Pheasant Tail. This rig imitates caddis larvae, Pale Morning Duns, and* Baetis *nymphs. In off-color water, I use a Bead-Head Buckskin. Later in the season, I'll drop a #20-22 RS2, Mercury Flashback Pheasant Tail, or Mercury Baetis off the Buckskin to imitate the fall caddis and* Baetis *nymphs.*

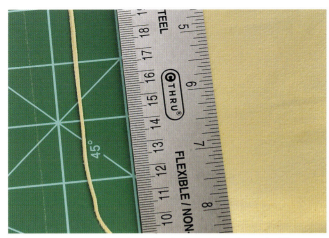

**5.** This is the preferred method of cutting chamois. You cannot make a precise cut with a pair of scissors. I recommend cutting several strips to save time at the vise. Cut varying widths so that you can tie sizes 16 through 20.

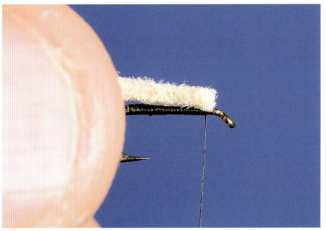

**6.** Take a chamois strip that is one-third the width of the hook gap. Lay your chamois strip on top of the shank, just behind the eye.

**7.** Secure the chamois strip with four tight wraps. Make sure the chamois does not spin on the hook.

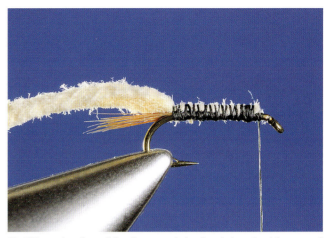

**8.** Wrap the thread back toward the hook bend with several tight wraps. Return to the initial tie in point of the chamois strip just behind the hook eye. These wraps need to be tight. Keep the abdomen as thin and uniform as possible.

**9.** Wrap the chamois strip forward toward the hook eye. Take extreme care to keep the wraps tight and next to each other. If the chamois strip keeps breaking, twist the chamois between your thumb and index finger prior to wrapping the strip. This will alleviate that problem.

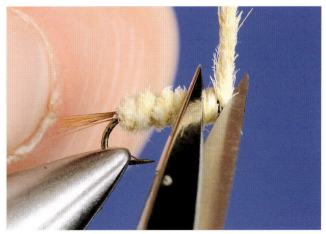

**10.** Hold the chamois strip with your left index finger and thumb at a 90-degree angle to the hook shank. Place your scissors on top of the hook shank and cut the excess chamois.

**11.** After the chamois strip has been trimmed, make several wraps of thread to bury the butt end of the chamois. At first, it may appear that you have crowded the head, but the chamois strip will compress easily to form a nice head.

**12.** The head should look like a miniature cone. Make two whip-finishes and clip thread.

**13.** Apply two drops of Doug's Head Cement on the head. Allow the head cement to penetrate into the chamois strip. Take a piece of copper wire and remove any cement in the eye. The key to a good Buckskin is keeping it thin and sparse. A prominent head is very important on this pattern.

### Bead-Head Buckskin

| | |
|---|---|
| Hook: | #16-20 Tiemco 2487 |
| Bead: | Brass ($\frac{3}{32}$" or 1.5mm) |
| Thread: | Tan 8/0 Uni-Thread |
| Body: | Thin chamois strip |

### Mercury Buckskin

| | |
|---|---|
| Hook: | #16-20 Tiemco 2487 |
| Bead: | Clear, silver-lined glass bead (extra small) |
| Thread: | Tan 8/0 Uni-Thread |
| Tail: | Brown hen hackle |
| Body: | Thin chamois strip |

# CHAPTER 17

# Puterbaugh Caddis

After a long, harsh winter in the Rocky Mountain region, April means longer days, warmer weather, and the promise of a new fishing season. In many drainages, anglers count down the days to the beginning of the Mother's Day Caddis hatch, which occurs during the latter part of April and first part of May. During this storied hatch, anglers celebrate the true beginning of spring with caddis festivals and other social gatherings. If flows and water temperatures are right, the Mother's Day Caddis hatch will provide the best dry-fly fishing of the year. Clouds of caddis fill the air, and scores of rising fish gorge themselves on the mothlike adults buzzing around the stream bank. This huge hatch benefits the ecosystem greatly—as much as 50 percent of a trout's yearly growth can occur during the latter part of April and first part of May.

The Puterbaugh Caddis has become my favorite fly to match the adults during this fabled hatch. Named after master fly tier and consummate angler Don Puterbaugh of Salida, Colorado, the Puterbaugh Caddis is one of the most versatile and durable caddis patterns ever fished. Puterbaugh has become a legend on the Arkansas River, spending upward of 250 days on the water each season, and has written several fly-tying books. He has several patterns with Umpqua Feather Merchants, but he is most known for his caddis. The Puterbaugh Caddis has fooled countless trout on the Arkansas drainage during the Mother's Day Caddis hatch each spring. After runoff subsides, trout continue to eagerly rise to this foam caddis, as sporadic caddis hatches remain an integral part of the trout's diet throughout the summer.

*Don Puterbaugh's foam caddis is an excellent choice during the famed Mother's Day Caddis hatch.*

*The Puterbaugh Caddis (lower right) is my favorite adult caddis pattern. It meets all the criteria for a good dry fly: it floats high in riffled water and is durable and easy to see.* JAY NICHOLS

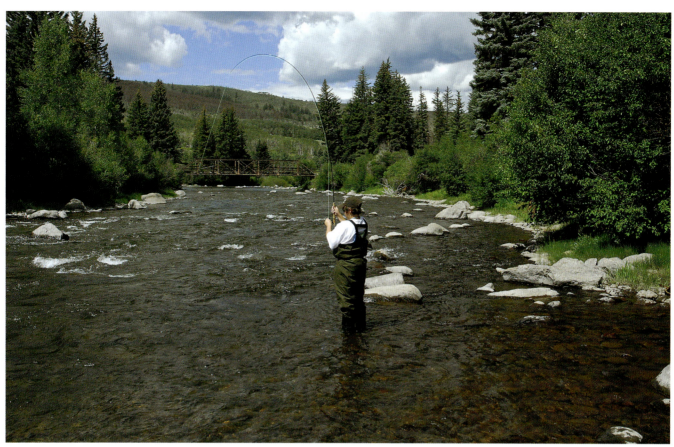

*Hunter Dorsey hooks a powerful Blue River rainbow that he fooled on a Puterbaugh Caddis.*

Puterbaugh developed the pattern in 1964 with the goal of creating a fly that was simple to tie and floated well. Because the fly is constructed from closed-cell foam, it floats like a cork. Puterbaugh recommends using 2mm foam for size 14, and 1.5mm foam for sizes 16-18. His second objective was to create a pattern that was easy to see. "I'm a firm believer in a wing you can see! That's why I tie this pattern with a light bull-elk wing, but not bleached because the elk hair is too brittle. The elk wing also assists in higher floatation," Puterbaugh said.

Your success during a caddis hatch is often the result of being in the right place at the right time. During mid to late

April, the water farthest from the source warms first, progressing slightly upriver each day. When the river reaches 54 degrees, caddis begin to emerge in huge numbers. If a cold snap occurs, the caddis hatch will stall until the water warms again (though you may have some good dry-fly fishing with Blue-Winged Olives, especially on overcast days).

Being on the leading edge of the hatch is one of the key ingredients for success. If you're fishing where the caddis concentration is the heaviest, your odds naturally drop, since trout are stuffed with both pupae and adults. In most cases, these trout are not as willing to eat as those fish on the front end of

*The Puterbaugh Caddis may be fished as a single dry fly or as an indicator fly in a dry-and-dropper rig. One of my favorite droppers is a #14-18 Mercer's Swing Nymph.*

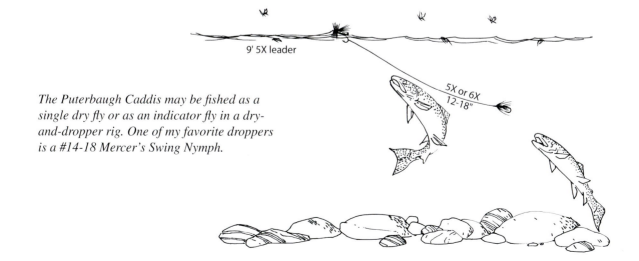

9' 5X leader

5X or 6X 12-18"

the hatch where the caddis activity is just getting started. The hatch moves quickly; in fact, it can move several miles in one day. Contact a local fly shop for up-to-date information before heading to the river.

## RIGGING AND FISHING TIPS

I typically fish the Puterbaugh Caddis with a 9-foot tapered leader, terminating in 5X. I most often fish it dead-drift, but occasionally I twitch or skate it, which can trigger explosive takes. If there is a dense hatch, I'll typically fish a Puterbaugh Caddis one size larger than the naturals to draw attention to the fly and help me distinguish the imposter from the blizzard of naturals.

The Puterbaugh Caddis also works well for a dry-and-dropper rig. In the initial phases of the hatch, I drop a caddis pupa, like LaFontaine's Sparkle Pupa, Bead-Head Breadcrust, or Mercer's Swing Nymph, on 18 to 24 inches of tippet off the bend of a Puterbaugh Caddis. This is an effective strategy for suspending caddis pupae that often drift for considerable distances in the upper part of the water column before emerging into adults. Once again, don't be afraid to let your flies swing in the current to entice strikes. Puterbaugh recommends applying dry-fly floatant to the elk wing and not the foam abdomen. He believes the treatment adds extra weight to the foam, compromising its floatability.

### Puterbaugh Caddis

| Hook: | #14-18 Tiemco 100 |
| Thread: | Black 8/0 Uni-Thread |
| Abdomen: | 1.5 or 2mm closed-cell foam |
| Wing: | Natural elk |
| Hackle: | Brown rooster |

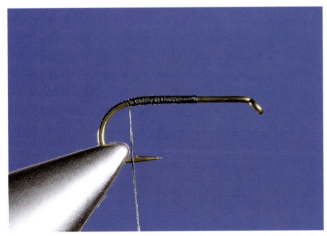

**1.** Place the hook in your vise, attach the thread at the midpoint of the hook shank, and wrap a smooth thread base to the hook bend.

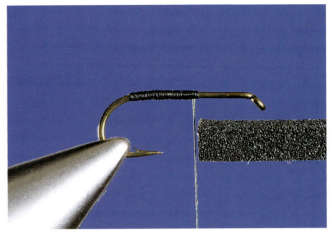

**2.** Return the thread to the midpoint, moving forward one thread width at a time to produce a smooth abdomen. Using a rotary cutter or straight edge and a self-healing cutting mat, cut a strip of closed-cell foam three-quarters of a hook gap wide.

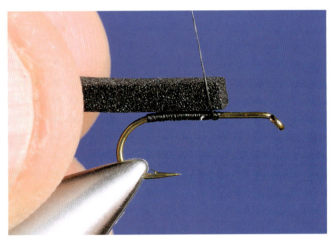

**3.** With your material hand's index finger and thumb, lay the closed-cell foam across the top of the hook shank. The foam should be attached slightly in front of the midpoint.

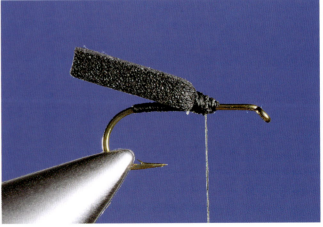

**4.** Secure the closed-cell foam with several wraps of thread. Smooth out the taper between the abdomen and the hook shank. Clip the butt end of the closed-cell foam so that it extends about three-quarters of a hook gap past the hook bend.

**5.** With your thumb and index finger, grab the tips of the elk hairs and cut the clump of hair as close to the hide as you can.

**8.** Pull the internal part of the hair stacker sideways from its base. The tips should be aligned and ready for the wing.

**6.** Hold the clump of elk hair in your left hand with your index finger and thumb. Sweep your right index finger back and forth to remove the unwanted underfur.

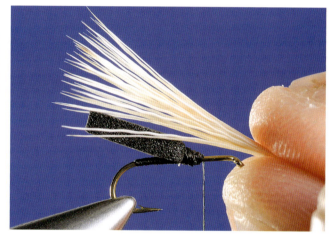

**9.** Pull the elk hair out of the stacker and transfer it to your other hand. The wing should be tied in so that it extends slightly beyond the abdomen.

**7.** After you remove the underfur, place the clump of elk hair into a hair stacker. Tap the hair stacker on your tying table a few times to align the tips.

**10.** Hold the elk with your material hand's index finger and thumb. Tie in the wing just past the tapered thread base in front of the abdomen. Make two wraps of thread with medium tension to snug down the hair and keep it bundled.

**11.** Directly in front of these gathering wraps, make a few more wraps to secure the hair, increasing pressure with each wrap to keep it from flaring. Trim the butts slightly in front of the tie-in point.

**12.** Bury the butt ends of the hair and smooth out the taper between the wing and the hook eye. Leave the thread in front of the wing.

**13.** Select a hackle from a rooster neck or saddle. Size it and strip the barbules from the stem. Tie the hackle in front of the wing with four tight wraps of thread.

**14.** Palmer the hackle forward from the base of the wing to the hook eye. This fly should be heavily hackled. Take four tight turns with the thread to secure the hackle.

**15.** Clip the extra hackle as close to the stem as possible and smooth out the head with several tight wraps of thread. Remove any stray or trapped hackle. Whip-finish and clip the thread. Apply one drop of head cement to the head. The Puterbaugh Caddis should have a slightly tilted foam abdomen that extends three-quarters of a hook gap beyond the hook bend. The elk wing should be on top of the foam and protrude slightly beyond the abdomen.

# CHAPTER 18

# *Paper Tiger*

Stoneflies rival mayflies in their diversity, with nearly six hundred species in the United States. It's rare to flip over a rock or sunken log and not find a stonefly or two, and a fast-water seine sample often reveals their prolific presence in streams with rocky bottoms. They thrive in fast, oxygenated riffles, runs, and pocketwater where opportunistic trout abound. The nymphs range in color from pale yellow to dark chocolate brown.

Stoneflies pass through an incomplete metamorphosis and are only available to trout during two stages: the prehistoric-looking nymph and the fluttering egg-laying adult. This greatly simplifies your fishing tactics and fly selection. The duration of each phase of their life cycle—egg, nymph, and adult—depends on the species and water temperatures. The smaller varieties generally have a one-year life span, whereas larger species such as the Golden Stone and Salmonfly (*Pteronarcys*) live three to four years.

During their seasonal emergence in the first two weeks of June, stonefly nymphs migrate toward the river's edge, crawling onto land to hatch into adults. Nymphing along the edges of the stream is very productive at this time. Stoneflies emerge once on land, and shucks on the tops of rocks, protruding logs, bridge abutments, and tree trunks will remove any doubt as to whether or not there are good populations of Golden Stones or *Pteronarcys* in the stream you are fishing.

I developed the brown Paper Tiger in the late 1980s to imitate the huge population of *Pteronarcys californica* nymphs in the Gunnison River. The Gunnison River is known for its

*Paper Tigers fish best in riffled water where the highest concentrations of stoneflies live.* JAY NICHOLS

*The Paper Tiger was designed to imitate the* Pteronarcys *stoneflies in the Gunnison River but works well in all rivers where these nymphs live.* JAY NICHOLS

*The yellow-brown version matches the abundant Golden Stone nymphs found on rivers across the country.* JAY NICHOLS

incredible nymphing with stonefly nymphs and excellent Salmonfly hatches. On most waters in the western United States, *Pteronarcys californica* hatches during the first two weeks of June, sometimes extending sporadically through early July, producing some of the best opportunities to catch big fish on big, juicy nymphs and bushy dry flies.

My primary goals in developing the Paper Tiger were to create a realistic and durable pattern. Tyvek, one of the key ingredients in the Paper Tiger, has been used for years in construction; in car, boat, and trailer covers; and in industrial packaging and envelopes. It creates a realistic abdomen, wing pads, and prothorax and offers superior durability from punctures, tears, and moisture, yet it easily accepts a permanent marker for coloration.

*Denver Post* columnist Charlie Meyers dubbed the fly the Paper Tiger. In an article he wrote about my stonefly, the caption for the fly read, "Paper Tiger: Pat Dorsey's Paper Stone offers the dual benefits of durability and ease in tying." The name stuck and the pattern has been known as the Paper Tiger for nearly twenty years. The yellow-brown Paper Tiger imitates *Hesperoperla pacifica*, or Golden Stone, which emerges mid-July to mid-August. The Golden Stone is the most prolific of all large stonefly species. Some of the best hatches occur in the Rocky Mountain region on both freestones and deep, bottom-release tailwaters. Because they crawl around so much, the nymphs are frequently swept away in the current, resulting in excellent nymphing with their imitations year-round.

Most of a stonefly's life is spent in the nymphal stage, so that is what trout eat the most. Because they have a multi-year life cycle, the nymphs remain abundant year-round, even after the mature stoneflies have emerged for the season. This means stoneflies can be effective even in the dead of winter. I have fished them for years in South Platte's Waterton Canyon with amazing results and have even seen tumbling chunks of anchor ice dislodge several stonefly nymphs, creating a small feeding frenzy.

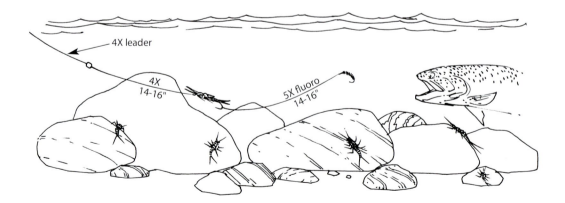

*A reliable rig when fishing stonefly nymphs is a Hydropsyche or mayfly nymph imitation tied to the bend of a Paper Tiger. Carry both weighted and unweighted versions for different water conditions.*

*Landon Mayer brings a 17-inch rainbow to the net. He caught the fish on a #8 brown Paper Tiger near Cooper Ranch on the Gunnison River.*

## RIGGING AND FISHING TIPS

I typically dead-drift my stonefly nymphs along the bottom in a conventional two-fly nymphing rig built from a 7½-foot tapered leader terminating in 3X or 4X. Since trout are not leader-shy when eating stoneflies, I use the thickest diameter leader I can get away with. When stoneflies are migrating toward shore to hatch into adults, concentrate your efforts along the river's edge. You will need to adjust your weight and strike indicator depth so that your flies occasionally tap on the bottom without getting hung up.

I carry weighted and unweighted versions in my fly boxes so that I can fish a wide array of structure, from mid-channel shelves to deeper holes and slots to fast, oxygenated pocket-water. The unweighted Paper Tigers fish best in the shallow riffles and water near the bank. I typically fish an unweighted version with one #4 split-shot to keep it bouncing along the bottom. Along with the stonefly, I'll typically fish a caddis, *Baetis* nymph, or Pale Morning Dun nymph.

In the higher flows of June and July runoff, fish upstream along the edges where the trout are holding and feeding in much shallower water than they might normally. As runoff peaks, the edges are traditionally the first to clear. This means that fish often become sensitive to overhead threats. Fishing straight upstream not only allows you to fish the bank water without wading too deep, but it also helps reduce the chances of spooking fish. Carefully work the bank water and then take a step or two upstream and repeat the process.

*Kim Dorsey enticed this Madison River rainbow to eat a Paper Tiger on a chilly spring day.*

## *Paper Tiger*

| Hook: | #4-10 Tiemco 300 |
|---|---|
| Thread: | Brown 6/0 Uni-Thread |
| Tail: | Black goose biots |
| Weight: | .030 lead wire |
| Underbody: | Brown yarn |
| Abdomen: | Tyvek strip |
| Legs: | Pheasant-tail fibers |
| Thorax: | Brown yarn |
| Wing Cases: | Tyvek strip |
| Antennae: | Black goose biots |

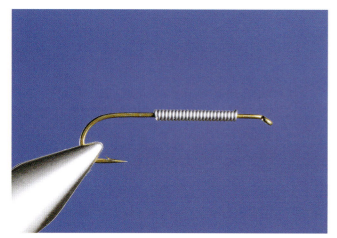

**1.** Place the hook into your vise. Make about 24 wraps of lead wire around the hook shank. Cut or break off the tag ends and slide the wire forward so that it is ³⁄₁₆ inch from the hook eye.

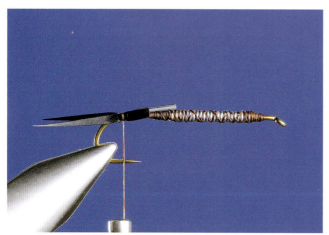

**2.** Attach the thread behind the lead wire and build a slight taper as you spiral-wrap the thread up to the lead wire. Wrap the thread back to a point just above the barb, and tie in two goose biots two-thirds the length of the hook shank.

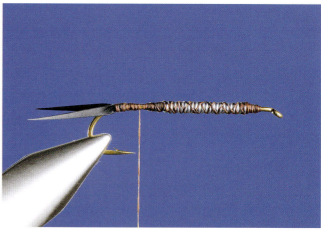

**3.** Trim the butt ends of the goose biots and smooth out the thread base.

**4.** Cut a 12-inch piece of yarn from the skein. Split and divide it into two sets of two strands each.

**5.** At the point shown above, attach the two strands of yarn with four tight wraps of thread.

**6.** Wrap the yarn back toward the hook bend and then wrap forward to the three-quarter point on the hook shank, developing a slight taper.

**7.** Clip the tag ends of the yarn and wrap the thread back to the hook point.

**8.** Slice a strip of Tyvek one hook gap wide with a rotary cutter or straight-edge and a self-healing cutting mat.

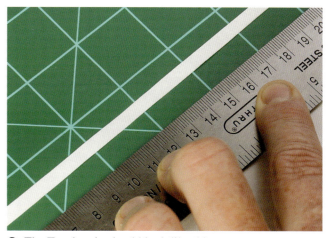

**9.** The Tyvek strip should look like this.

**10.** Tie in the strip of Tyvek with six tight wraps of thread.

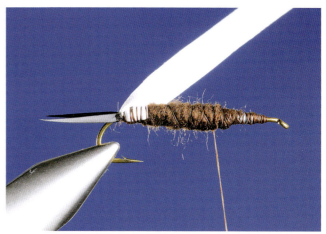

**11.** Wrap the thread forward to the point shown. Pull the Tyvek strip forward at a 45-degree angle.

**12.** With your material hand's thumb and index finger, wrap the Tyvek strip forward to produce a segmented abdomen.

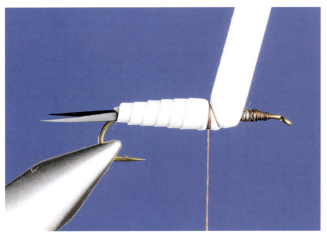

**13.** Tie off the Tyvek strip and secure it with four tight wraps of thread.

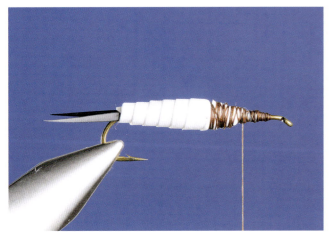

**14.** Trim the tag end of the Tyvek strip and smooth out the thread base between the hook shank and abdomen. Secure the thread with a half-hitch.

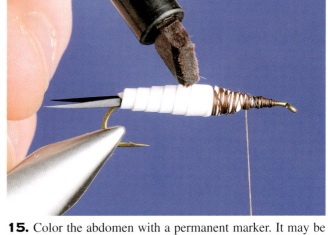

**15.** Color the abdomen with a permanent marker. It may be necessary to coat the abdomen twice.

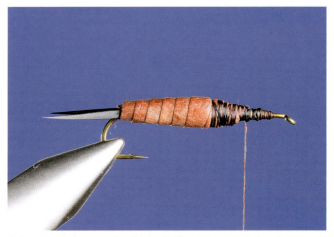

**16.** The abdomen should look like this after it has been colored.

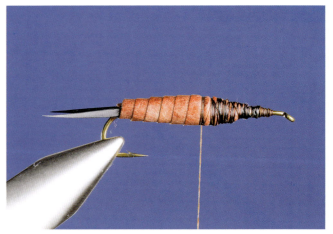

**17.** Wrap the thread back to midshank and make four tight wraps to secure the thread.

**18.** Attach a single strand of yarn and wrap the thread forward to the point shown above.

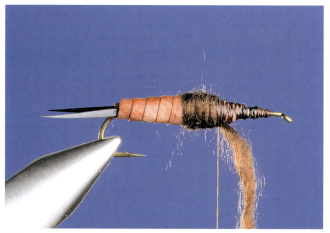

**19.** Wrap the yarn on the shank to form a smooth base on which to affix the legs. The yarn base should be about one hook gap wide.

**20.** Select 10 to 12 pheasant-tail fibers from the center tail feather. Align the tips and tie in the leg farthest away from you first with four tight wraps of thread. The leg should be tied in on the side of the abdomen. The tips should extend to the end of the abdomen.

**21.** Tie in the leg closest to you with four tight wraps of thread.

**22.** Clip the butts of the pheasant-tail fibers and secure them with several wraps of thread. Wrap the thread beyond the first yarn base.

**23.** Tie in another single strand of yarn, leaving the thread hanging at the tie-in point.

**24.** Wrap the yarn back over the thread wraps, covering the tie-in point of the first set of legs.

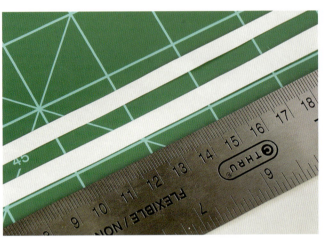

**25.** To create the wing pads, slice another piece of Tyvek slightly wider than the one you used for the abdomen.

**26.** Cut a notch into the Tyvek strip with a sharp pair of scissors. Make the first cut as shown, cutting at a 45-degree angle from the corner to the midpoint of the Tyvek strip. Rest the scissors on your fingers for a precise cut.

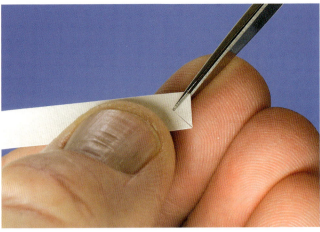

**27.** The second cut comes in from the opposing corner and meets the first at the midpoint of the Tyvek strip.

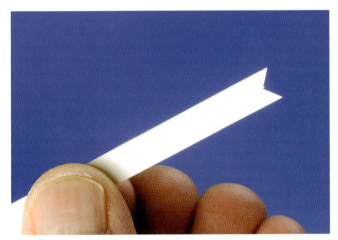

**28.** Top view of the notched Tyvek strip.

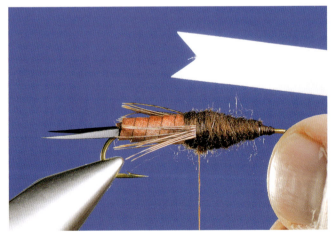

**29.** Clip the yarn and leave the thread hanging in front of the first set of legs.

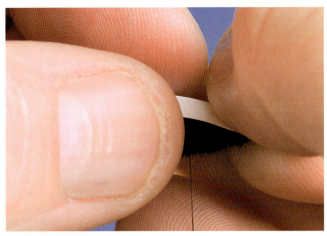

**30.** Using both hands, lay the notched Tyvek strip on top of the shank. Pinch the Tyvek strip with your left index thumb and finger to hold it in place.

**31.** The Tyvek strip should be tied in just beyond the first set of legs with four tight wraps of thread. Each wrap of thread needs to be on top of the preceeding wrap.

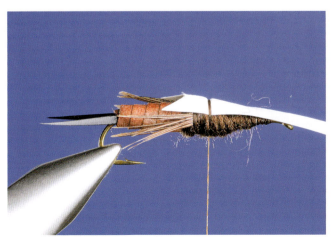

**32.** This is what the first wing pad should look like. The tight wraps of thread actually lift the wing case slightly off the abdomen.

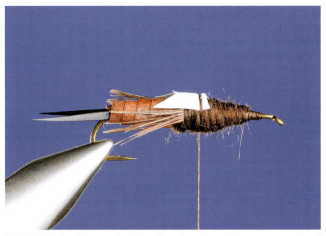

**33.** Clip the butt end of the Tyvek strip with a sharp pair of scissors.

**34.** Top view of first wing pad.

**35.** Tie in the second pair of legs at the tie-off point of the first wing pad. The tips of the legs should extend to the middle of the first legs.

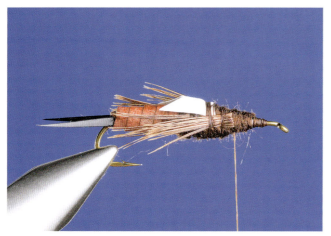

**36.** Clip the butt ends of the pheasant-tail fibers and secure them with several tight wraps of thread.

**37.** Tie in another single strand of yarn to hide the thread you used to tie in the wing case and second set of legs. Smooth out the taper of the thorax and tie off the yarn with four tight wraps of thread.

**38.** Clip the tag end of the yarn. Select another strip of Tyvek and notch it like the first wing pad. Lay the second wing pad on top of the hook shank and secure it with four tight wraps of thread. The spacing between the wing pads should be equivalent to the segment spacing on the abdomen. Do not cut off the butt end of the Tyvek strip.

**39.** Pull the Tyvek strip back at a 45-degree angle.

**40.** Tie in the third set of legs in front of the second wing pad. The tips of the legs should extend to the middle of the second set of legs.

**41.** Tie in a single strand of yarn behind the hook eye and cover up the butt ends of the pheasant-tail fibers and any visible thread wraps. Leave the thread just in front of the third set of legs.

**42.** Pull the Tyvek strip over the thorax so that it extends over the hook eye. Make four tight wraps between the tie-in point of the second wing pad and the hook eye to form the third wing case.

**43.** Wrap the thread forward toward the hook eye. Wrap the thread around the hook eye one time to hold it in place.

**44.** Pull the Tyvek strip tight and make four tight wraps of thread behind the hook eye to create the prothorax.

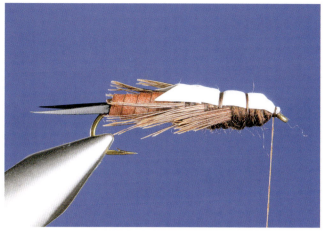

**45.** Trim the Tyvek strip as close as you can to the hook eye.

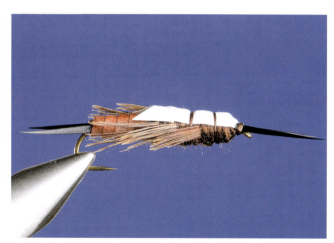

**46.** Tie in a goose biot on each side of the head for antennae. The antennae should be half a hook shank long.

**47.** Top view of the wing cases and antennae.

**48.** Color the wing cases and prothorax with a permanent marker. A top view of the finished fly is shown above. The tail should be two-thirds the length of the shank and the abdomen should be slightly tapered. The legs should span the back two-thirds of the hook shank, and the wing cases and prothorax should cover approximately half of the hook shank. The antennae should be slightly longer than the tail. Be careful not to crowd the head; otherwise you'll have difficulty tying in the antennae.

**49.** The tying steps for the Golden Stone variation are exactly the same. The preparation of the materials varies, however. On a piece of cardboard, color a piece of Tyvek with yellow permanent marker.

**50.** Flip the Tyvek strip over and make one or two quick strokes over the back side with the brown marker.

**51.** Be careful not to overdo it. One quick stroke over the Tyvek trip is adequate.

**52.** The brown marker seeps through the yellow side producing a mottled effect.

### *Golden Paper Tiger*

| | |
|---|---|
| Hook: | #8-12 Tiemco 300 |
| Thread: | Brown 6/0 Uni-Thread |
| Tail: | Gold goose biots |
| Weight: | .020 lead wire |
| Underbody: | Gold yarn |
| Abdomen: | Tyvek strip |
| Legs: | Pheasant-tail fibers |
| Thorax: | Gold yarn |
| Wing Cases: | Tyvek strip |
| Antennae: | Gold goose biots |

# CHAPTER 19

# *Amy's Ant*

Amy's Ant was developed by master angler and fly tier Jack Dennis of Jackson, Wyoming. This beautiful dry fly has become a favorite adult stonefly imitation for anglers and guides alike because it fools hard-fished trout under a wide range of conditions. According to Dennis, his wife and former vice president Dick Cheney inspired him to tie this fly for the famous Jackson Hole One Fly. Before designing the fly, Dennis asked several guides in the Jackson area for their input on how they would improve the famed Chernobyl Ant. James Osborne, head guide of Heise Outfitters, and several other colleagues offered their input. According to Dennis, "It was really everybody's fly, as I borrowed a suggestion or two from a multitude of friends to craft the final product."

After a group consensus, one of the biggest problems with the Chernobyl Ant was that it lacked a wing to imitate the natural movement of an adult stonefly. Taking suggestions from veteran guides, Dennis decided to design an underwing from rainbow Krystal Flash, which would glow from the light through the water to imitate fluttering wings. Dennis later added a tan elk-hair wing on top of the Krystal Flash to add buoyancy, and pulled the front foam back into the thorax to form a wing case. This produced a durable fly that floated like a cork and rode high on fast currents.

Dennis says, "The best judge was the fish. We caught an amazing number of fish the first time we started fishing the fly. It won the One Fly in 1999 and quickly became vice president

*Amy's Ant has taken Western waters by storm. Invented by Jack Dennis and popularized by Monroe Coleman, Amy's Ant has become many anglers' favorite dry fly.* JAY NICHOLS

*Big rainbows in Cheesman Canyon take Amy's Ant with confidence. Bob Dye and Jeff Hutchens are all smiles after landing this beauty near Monroe's Rock in the lower part of Cheesman Canyon.*

*Amy's Ant was designed to imitate adult Golden Stones, which hatch for a three- to four-week period starting in late June or early July.*

Cheney's favorite fly." The pattern was later named Amy's Ant, after Dennis' daughter.

Monroe Coleman, a veteran guide of 20-plus years for the Blue Quill Angler, popularized Amy's Ant in Colorado, specifically in Cheesman Canyon where there is a robust population of Golden Stones. Word spread quickly, and Amy's Ant has become a favorite fly on the Blue, Gunnison, Williams Fork, Colorado, Eagle, and many other Colorado rivers.

Amy's Ant is versatile and fishes well as a single dry fly or as an indicator fly in a dry-and-dropper rig. It can be fished in a variety of colors—red, yellow, orange, black, and olive—to imitate adult stoneflies, crickets, hoppers, or any other big terrestrial. I've enjoyed my best success with the olive variation. Natural Golden Stone adults have a brilliant yellow-olive sheen that is perfectly portrayed by Amy's Ant. Toss in the fluttering elk wing and rubber legs for lifelike movement, and you have the perfect dry fly for stoneflies.

## RIGGING AND FISHING TIPS

I generally fish Amy's Ant with a 9-foot tapered leader terminating in 4X. Amy's Ant fishes best between June and September. To be successful, cover the water methodically,

*One of my favorite rigs is a #18-20 tungsten bead Mercer's Micro Mayfly tied to the bend of an Amy's Ant on 18 to 24 inches of tippet.*

showing your fly to as many fish as possible. If you see a splashy rise that might indicate a trout is feeding on adult stoneflies, cast to it—but it's rare to find any type of regular feeding pattern when you're fishing adult stoneflies. Concentrate your efforts around darker areas in the substrate and shallow riffles on the stream bank. Especially target water close to logs, cliff faces, and partially submerged structure where stoneflies routinely fall into the water. Fishing water that is 2 to 4 feet deep will produce the best results.

I dead-drift Amy's Ant most of the time. At times, however, imparting action to the fly will trigger explosive strikes, so don't be afraid to experiment. One of the most common mistakes when fishing large dry flies is setting the hook too early. Allow the trout to come up, eat your fly, and dip its head below the surface before you gently lift the rod tip to set the hook. If you react prematurely, you may come away empty-handed. If you miss your target, the chances are pretty good you have spoiled your opportunity; however, I have switched to a red variation and enticed the trout to rise again.

Using Amy's Ant as an indicator in a dry-and-dropper rig is deadly and allows you to fish a wide assortment of water, including shallow bank water, transitional zones that funnel into deep pools, riffles, runs, and pocketwater. Most importantly, it allows you to fish skinny water that rarely gets fished with a conventional nymphing rig.

### Amy's Ant (Olive)

| | |
|---|---|
| Hook: | #4-8 Tiemco 5263 |
| Thread: | Brown 6/0 Uni-Thread |
| Underbody: | Tan foam |
| Overbody: | Brown foam |
| Legs: | Brown rubber (medium) |
| Hackle: | Brown |
| Body: | Olive Krystal Chenille |
| Wing: | Light elk hair over rainbow Krystal Flash |
| Thorax: | Arizona peacock dubbing |

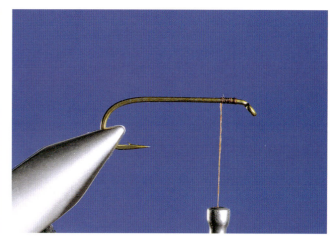

**1.** Clamp the hook into the vise. Attach the thread at the 90-percent point on the hook shank and clip the tag end.

*This brown trout was fooled by Amy's Ant during a Golden Stone hatch. Amy's Ant is also an effective attractor through the summer and fall.* JAY NICHOLS

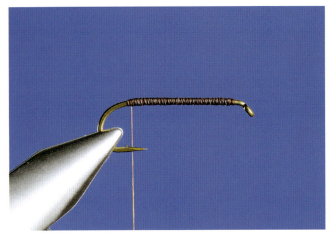

**2.** Create a uniform thread base that extends to the hook bend. This provides a solid foundation for the remaining materials, ensuring they will not spin on the hook shank when you tie them in.

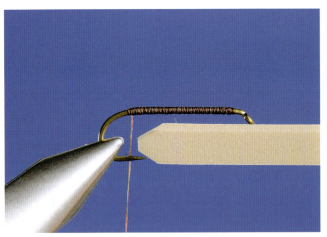

**3.** Cut a strip of tan closed-cell foam one hook gap wide with a rotary cutter or straight-edge and self-healing cutting mat. Trim the corners. Use a sharp pair of scissors for a clean cut.

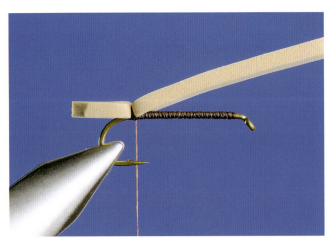

**4.** Tie in the foam strip at a point just above the barb with three to four wraps. The foam strip should extend beyond the hook bend one third of a shank length.

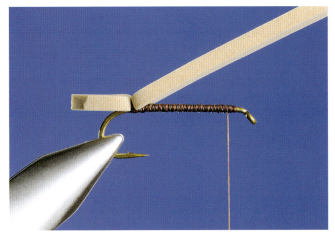

**5.** Wrap the thread to the front of the hook, keeping the thread underbody uniform.

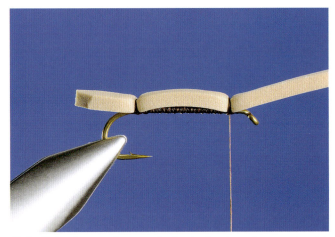

**6.** Pull the foam strip over the hook shank and secure it with three to four wraps of thread ⅛ inch behind the hook eye.

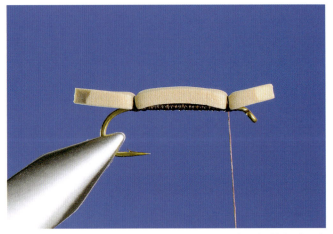

**7.** Trim the foam strip so that a length equal to half the hook gap extends beyond the hook eye.

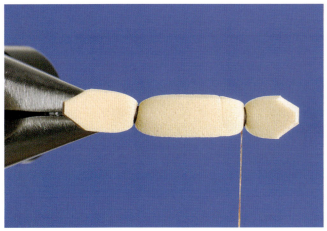

**8.** Trim the corners with sharp scissors. The squared-off front edge should be about a third of the foam strip.

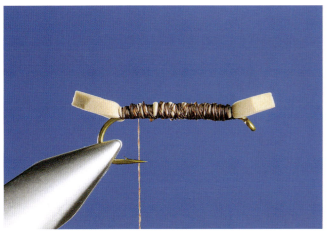

**9.** Wrap the thread back and forth along the shank to compress the foam strip and stop the thread just in front of the barb.

**10.** With your thumb and middle finger, strip away $\frac{1}{8}$ inch of the Krystal Chenille, exposing the center core. Tie in the Krystal Chenille with four wraps of thread, and wrap the thread back to a point just above the barb.

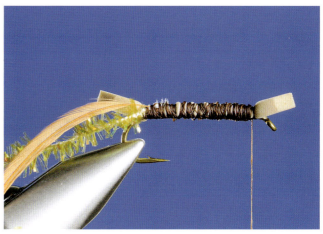

**11.** Size a rooster hackle with barbules equal to the hook gap. Tie it in dull side up, and wrap the thread forward to the front tie-in point of the foam.

**12.** Wrap the Krystal Chenille forward, secure it with three wraps of thread, and clip the excess. The Krystal Chenille should not extend beyond the front tie-in point of the foam strip.

**13.** Palmer the hackle forward and tie it off behind the foam strip. Keep the wraps about $\frac{1}{16}$ inch apart.

**14.** Wrap the thread back through the palmered hackle.

**15.** Pre-trim the rubber legs to one shank length. Tie in the first rubber leg with two wraps of thread.

**16.** Fold the second leg around the thread.

**17.** Slide the rubber leg up the thread, positioning it across from the first leg. Make sure the leg is on the side of the abdomen. You can adjust the angle of the legs with thread tension. Keep the legs at a 45-degree angle to the hook shank.

**18.** Release the rubber leg from your thumb and index finger. Make three wraps to secure the rear legs.

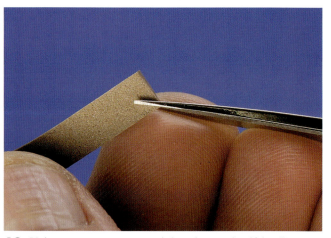

**19.** Using a rotary cutter, straight-edge, and self-healing cutting mat, cut a strip of brown closed-cell foam slightly wider than the underbody foam. Hold the foam with your thumb and index finger. Resting the scissors on your fingers, make a precise cut about ⅛ inch into the foam.

**20.** The cut should look like this.

**21.** Tie in the foam so that it extends slightly past the underbody foam. Secure the foam strip with three turns of thread. The foam strip should be propped slightly. You can adjust the angle of the foam with thread tension.

**22.** Wrap the thread forward, retracing the hackle wraps.

**23.** Pull the foam strip over the hook shank and secure it with two wraps of thread in the same position as the underbody foam.

**24.** Create a thread base to tie in the wing and front legs without creating excessive bulk. Don't worry about being neat. You will cover this with dubbing.

**25.** Tie in approximately 25 strands of rainbow Krystal Flash for the underwing. They should extend to the back of the upper foam strip. Clip the butt ends of the Krystal Flash and cover them with thread, keeping bulk to a minimum.

**26.** With your thumb and index finger, grab a clump of yearling elk hair. Yearling elk hair is softer and has a thinner wall diameter than bull or cow elk hair, which makes it compress very easily. Cut the clump of hair as close to the hide as possible.

**27.** Hold the tips of the elk hair in your left hand and use your right index finger to remove the underfur and short fibers with a back-and-forth sweeping movement.

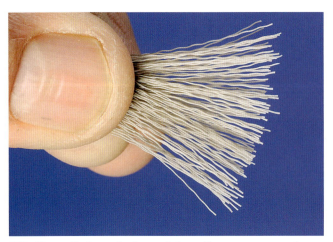

**28.** Once all the underfur and short fibers are removed, you are ready to stack the hair and align the tips.

**29.** This is what the tips should look like after they have been stacked. If there are any broken tips, remove them now.

**30.** After removing the yearling elk hair from the hair stacker, place the elk hair on top of the underwing. The length of the wing should be equal to the length of the brown foam. Be careful not to flare the wing excessively with too much thread tension. The wing should be slightly wider than the brown foam.

**31.** Clip the butt ends of the elk hair and even out the thread wraps. Use a drop or two of head cement to secure the wing.

**32.** Dub over the tie-in point of the wing. Because these dubbing fibers are short, they are difficult to work with. Use dubbing wax and small quantities of dubbing to form your noodle.

**33.** Tie in the front legs with two wraps of thread. They should be one shank length long.

**34.** Tie in the second leg on the other side with two wraps of thread. Pull the foam strip back over the hook shank and secure it with three wraps of thread.

**35.** Wrap the thread forward, taking two wraps between the brown and tan foam. Hold the rubber legs with your fingers to keep them from getting trapped when making these wraps.

**36.** With your thumb and index finger, pull back the tan foam and legs and make two wraps of thread.

**37.** The fly should look like this.

**38.** Whip-finish, and trim the foam strip. The first cut should be across the hook shank at a 90-degree angle followed by two cuts to trim the corners and form a point.

**39.** The finished fly. The top view shows the correct proportions of the legs, wing, and prothorax area. Amy's Ant has multiple tying steps, which can make it difficult to get the correct proportions. The most important concerns are that the brown foam extends slightly beyond the tan foam, the length of the underwing equals the length of the brown foam, and the elk-hair wing extends slightly beyond the underwing. Do not crowd the head; otherwise you'll have difficulty tying off the wing case and whip-finishing the fly.

### Amy's Ant (Red)

| | |
|---|---|
| Hook: | #4-8 Tiemco 5263 |
| Thread: | Black 6/0 Uni-Thread |
| Underbody: | Light-pink foam |
| Overbody: | Black foam |
| Legs: | Black rubber (medium) |
| Hackle: | Grizzly |
| Body: | Red Krystal Chenille |
| Wing: | Light elk hair over rainbow Krystal Flash |
| Thorax: | Red dubbing |

# CHAPTER 20

# Nuclear Egg

Egg imitations are most effective during the spring and fall when trout are spawning and natural eggs are rolling along the stream bottom. Many anglers have an inner struggle with fishing egg patterns because they associate them with bait. I run across several anglers each season who refuse to fish with egg patterns and San Juan Worms, but those anglers are limiting their success.

I believe our job as anglers is to match the prevailing food organisms that are available to trout on any given day of the year, whether that is fishing a Black Beauty in January to imitate midges or fishing a stonefly nymph near the bank in June. If the fish are spawning and eggs are available to trout, I'll match the hatch and fish egg patterns. If the name of the game is to catch trout, why limit your success?

Traditionally rainbows, cuttbows, and cutthroat spawn in the spring and brook and brown trout spawn in the fall. Over the past few seasons, I have observed more fall spawning rainbows with the recent crossbreeding and stocking conducted by game and fish agencies. I also believe that the time of year these fingerlings are stocked has a profound effect on when they spawn. For instance, if the rainbows or cuttbows are stocked in the fall, they will spawn in the fall. Rainbows tend to spawn over a several-month period, starting as early as mid-February and continuing until mid-June, depending on water temperatures. Brown trout as a whole tend to have a shorter spawning window, traditionally with the bulk of their activity occurring in a three- to four-week period starting mid-October and lasting until the first or second week of November. On

*The Nuclear Egg is one of the most realistic egg patterns that I have ever fished. It looks unconvincing when it is in the vise, but get it wet and it's a winner.* JAY NICHOLS

*Cody Scott caught this awesome rainbow with an egg pattern on the Blue River in the town of Silverthorne.*

*Top: Bob Dye regularly uses an egg pattern as an attractor in his two-fly nymphing rigs. He uses a mayfly dropper in the spring and fall and midges in the winter.*

*Josh Behr landed this stunning brown trout during the annual spawning run above Elevenmile Reservoir. As a whole, anglers generally target these pre-spawn fish with egg patterns. The Nuclear Egg is an excellent choice during the latter part of September through October.*

certain watersheds like the Bighorn below Yellowtail Dam, brown trout may spawn as late as December.

Don't fish to trout on redds, which are the scoured-out bowl-like depressions where the fish actually lay and fertilize the eggs. Redds are lighter in color than the rest of the substrate. Targeting trout on redds hurts the natural recruitment of younger fish. As stewards of the environment, we must protect these spawners and let them propagate with the least amount of stress possible.

My favorite egg pattern is the Nuclear Egg. While guiding for steelhead on Michigan's Betsie River, Walt Grau, from the Pere Marquette Lodge, kept noticing colored yarn clippings on the snow near the river's edge. One day Grau stumbled upon a steelheader who was adding yarn to spawn that was already on a snelled hook. This angler was inserting the yarn into a monofilament loop and consistently catching fish. That evening Grau took that concept to his tying vise, and the Nuclear Egg was born. It is the most realistic egg pattern I've ever fished.

*I carry an assortment of egg patterns. One of my favorites has always been the Nuclear Egg (middle).*

The Nuclear Egg was later introduced to Colorado angler Bob Kennedy—a Michigan native and close friend of Grau's—who sent two dozen to his close friend Roger Bittell, a guide from the Blue Quill Angler. Bittell is credited with popularizing the Nuclear Egg in the Rocky Mountain area by distributing samples to several Blue Quill Angler guides. Word spread quickly, and today the Nuclear Egg is a staple.

### RIGGING AND FISHING TIPS

I typically fish my egg patterns with a 7-foot, 3X to 4X tapered leader terminating in 3X to 5X fluorocarbon. Fish that are keying on eggs are not leader shy, so use the heaviest tippet you can get away with. Clarity is your biggest consideration. In clear water, use 5X; in off-color water, 3X or 4X. I rarely fish my egg patterns with anything less than 4X, unless I'm not getting strikes. The larger tippet allows you to persuade big trout away from structure that may potentially cause you to lose your trophy. Lake-run trout may run up to 10 to 12 pounds, and it's comforting to know you have a good chance of landing them with the heavier tippet.

I tie Nuclear Eggs in burnt orange, pink, and chartreuse. Chartreuse eggs have saved the day for me in high and muddy water, and I have a tremendous amount of confidence in them. I have found that Kamloops rainbows and brook trout are especially fond of eating chartreuse Nuclear Eggs under a wide range of conditions.

4X leader

4X or 5X fluoro
14–16"

6X
14–16"

*Egg-and-midge combos are one of my favorite rigs during the winter. The egg draws attention to the smaller midge, a predominant food organism at that time. During the spawning season (February and March, and then again in October and November), I'll typically fish my eggs with a Flashback Mercury RS2, Sparkle Wing RS2, or a Mercury Flashback Pheasant Tail because the trout key on Baetis nymphs. I tend to fish them in the faster riffles and slots where fish are holding deep but are occasionally eating eggs that may have drifted away from nearby spawning flats.*

Black Beauty (winter)

RS2 and Mercury PT (early spring and fall)

## *Nuclear Egg*

| | |
|---|---|
| Hook: | #14-16 Tiemco 2457 |
| Thread: | Orange 6/0 Danville |
| Nucleus: | Dark-orange McFly Foam |
| Halo: | Candy cane, egg, or white Glo Bug Yarn |

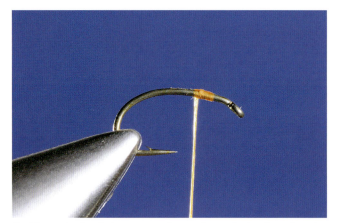

**1.** Place the hook into your vise and attach the thread at the point shown above.

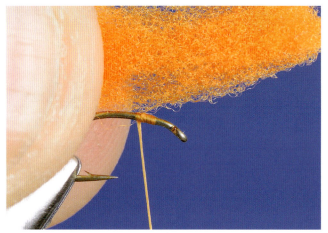

**2.** Remove the orange McFly Foam from its package. Peel away one strand of foam from the main bundle. This will be used to create the embryo of the egg.

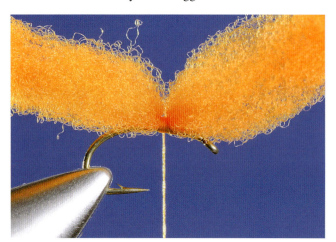

**3.** Secure the McFly Foam with six tight wraps of thread. Leave the thread hanging behind the embryo.

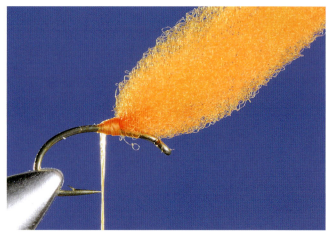

**4.** Trim the butt ends of the McFly Foam and smooth out the taper between the hook shank and the embryo.

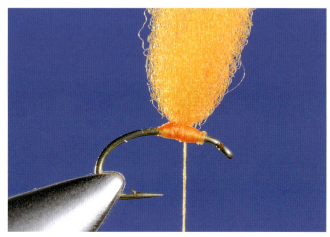

**5.** With your material hand, prop up the yarn and build a thread wedge in front of the embryo. Smooth out the taper on both sides of the yarn.

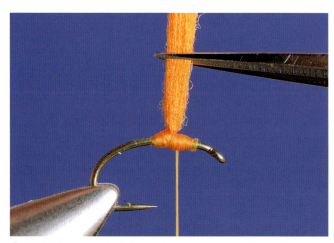

**6.** Pull the yarn straight up to tighten the McFly Foam and trim the embryo to length (one hook gap).

**7.** The trimmed embryo should look like this.

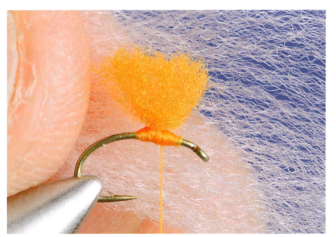

**8.** Pull out a piece of Glo Bug Yarn from the package. Separate one strand into thirds. With your thumb and index finger of each hand, spread the Glo Bug Yarn out so that it lays flat. This will be used for the halo.

**9.** Hold the flattened piece of Glo Bug Yarn vertically on the outside edge of the hook shank with the thumb and index finger of your material hand. Make a counter-clockwise, loose wrap around the yarn.

**10.** Pull the bobbin straight down and take three additional tight wraps to secure the Glo Bug Yarn.

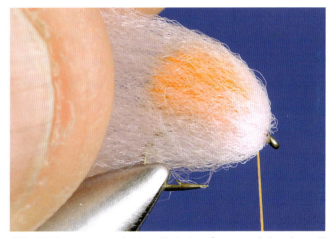

**11.** With your material hand's index finger and thumb, pull back the remaining piece of Glo Bug Yarn and pinch the material behind the hook bend. Leave the thread hanging behind the hook eye.

**12.** Hold the Glo Bug Yarn in place and smooth out the head. There should be a slight taper between the hook eye and the halo.

**13.** Whip-finish and clip the thread. Apply two drops of head cement to the head.

**14.** With the thumb and fingers of your material hand, pull back the Glo Bug Yarn and trim the halo behind the embryo.

**15.** This fly might look funny when it is dry, but when it is submersed it looks very realistic. The orange embryo should extend to the hook bend and the halo should conform to the embryo and extend slightly beyond it.

### *Nuclear Egg (Chartreuse)*

| | |
|---|---|
| Hook: | #14-16 Tiemco 2457 |
| Thread: | Chartreuse 6/0 Danville |
| Nucleus: | Chartreuse McFly Foam |
| Halo: | Candy cane, egg, or white Glo Bug Yarn |

### *Nuclear Egg (Pink)*

| | |
|---|---|
| Hook: | #14-16 Tiemco 2457 |
| Thread: | Pink 6/0 Danville |
| Nucleus: | Pink McFly Foam |
| Halo: | Candy cane, egg, or white Glo Bug Yarn |

# CHAPTER 21

# UV Scud

My first memorable experience with scud patterns occurred on the beautiful Green River below Flaming Gorge Dam nearly 25 years ago. My fishing partner Harold Tygart and I heard anglers ranting and raving about the huge fish they were catching between the Little Hole access and the dam. We decided to load up the car and go see for ourselves what the hype was about.

In preparation, Tygart and I tied a bunch of scuds in three different colors—tan (a mixture of 19 and 20 Ligas dubbing that was referred as a 19½ scud), olive, and orange. We stuffed our fly boxes with dozens of scuds prior to our departure to the Flaming Gorge Lodge.

Tygart and I pulled into the Little Hole parking lot, parked, and walked upstream for several miles into the boulder-filled canyon, sight-fishing to large fish positioned in the transitional zones that dumped into some of the deeper runs. From a high vantage point, you could see monsters lurking in the depths of some of the deeper holes. It was like an aquarium—fish were everywhere. Both Tygart and I had trout readily intercepting our scud imitations, especially the 19½ scud. That day we did not hook and land any trophies, but we did catch a bunch of 14- to 18-inch fish, and it was an eye-opening experience to learn how effective scuds can be under the right circumstances.

Closer to home, I found the South Platte to have a dense population of scuds. My friend Randy Smith has always had a tremendous amount of success in Cheesman Canyon with scuds, especially in May and June when the water levels rise from runoff. His nickname is "Scud Mo" because he can

*The UV Scud can be tied in a variety of colors by simply switching the color of your dubbing. My favorite colors include orange, olive, pale olive, and tan.* JAY NICHOLS

*UV Scuds are effective during higher flows on many Western tailwaters, and during low-light periods when naturals become more active and vulnerable to predation. They also work well as egg imitations during the spring and fall.*
LANDON MAYER

*Brad Coors hooked and landed this huge Spinney Mountain Ranch rainbow on an orange UV Scud.*

always entice a trout to eat one of his scud offerings. After watching Smith nymph Cheesman Canyon, I become a believer in scuds, too. It was a sight to see—he nailed fish after fish in one of the toughest rivers in the West.

Scuds thrive in streams and rivers with slow to moderate currents and dense beds of aquatic vegetation. Since they prefer consistent flows and stable water temperatures, they often thrive in tailwaters. Of the approximately ninety species of scuds in North America, the most important genus to fly fishers is *Gammarus*. *Gammarus lacustris* is an olive scud that is most abundant in the waters I fish. Scuds are effective year-round, especially on weed-rich tailwaters such as the South

Platte, Bighorn, Green, and Colorado at Lee's Ferry, where thick-bodied trout grow fast and sport magnificent colors from their scud-heavy diets.

Scuds have a flat, segmented abdomen, 14 pairs of legs, a glossy looking shellback, two pairs of antennae, and a tail. They are excellent swimmers and are often found moving about in dense beds of aquatic vegetation. Scud patterns tend to be most effective during higher flows when the naturals get dislodged from the river bottom.

I recommend tying up a bunch of scuds in gray-olive, tan, and orange. Most of the scuds you'll encounter will be gray-olive. Gray-olive scuds represent living scuds; orange scuds

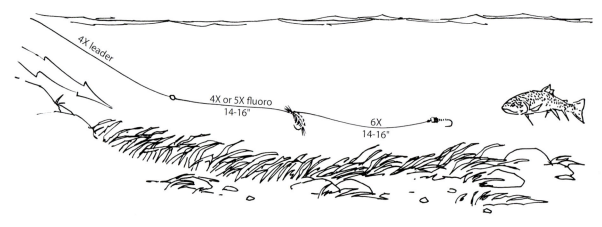

*Off the eye of a UV Scud, I typically tie a midge pattern like the Mercury Black Beauty or Mercury Blood Midge on 14 to 16 inches of 5X or 6X fluorocarbon. Add split-shot 14 to 16 inches in front of the scud.*

imitate dead scuds; and tan scuds, from what I am told, imitate molting scuds. On occasion, you might see a scud with an orange spot in the middle of its abdomen. This is a pregnant female with a brood pouch. Trout key on pregnant scuds at times, so it is a good idea to carry a few to imitate them. You can imitate this brood pouch by adding a small ball of orange dubbing on the hook shank. Scuds may molt (shed their old shell and replace it with a new, shinier one) anywhere from 15 to 20 times. Roger Hill, author of *Fly Fishing the South Platte* and one of Colorado's best anglers, has told me that trout like to eat them when they are molting because they are soft and easy to eat.

In my seine samples, I find about 99 percent gray-olive scuds with a few tan ones. To date, I have never seined an orange scud. My stomach-pump analysis, however, reveals another story. It shows all three colors, but it's hard to determine whether a trout ate a dead scud (orange) or an olive scud that turned orange in the trout's belly after it perished. While most evidence proves that gray-olive are most abundant, I have caught considerably more trout on orange scuds.

In fisheries like the Colorado River at Lees Ferry, where hydroelectrical commitments cause erratic flows, scuds are left "high and dry" after peak generation occurs and the flow recedes. The next day when the flow rises again, huge numbers of dead, orange scuds are knocked loose, and the fish capitalize on this easy feeding opportunity. On a smaller scale, this occurs with bottom-release tailwaters, where releases frequently occur to meet irrigation demands downstream. Scouring flows from flow increases frequently knock loose both dead and living scuds, causing a smorgasbord for the trout.

Orange scuds can also be good egg imitations, and I've had a tremendous amount of success on the Bighorn with scuds in March and April. Although stomach samples prove that Bighorn trout eat huge numbers of dead scuds, it is entirely possible they are taking the orange scud as an egg. At this time, many of the rainbow trout are spawning in some of the back channels and other shallow areas.

## RIGGING AND FISHING TIPS

I generally use a scud as an attractor in a two-fly nymphing rig and drop a small mayfly or midge below it. I have had the best success fishing scuds in transitional zones that dump into deeper slots and holes, especially below thick weed beds where trout are accustomed to seeing scuds. I generally use a 9-foot leader tapered to 4X because the takes are usually aggressive. On some watersheds like Cheesman Canyon, I dredge my scuds, while on the Bighorn, I typically use one or two #4 split-shots, experimenting until I find what works best.

*Mike O'Leary nymphs the famed Ice Box in Cheesman Canyon with an orange UV Scud. During higher flows, scuds are routinely knocked loose from the substrate and become an important part of the trout's diet.*

*I keep a box stuffed with an assortment of UV Scuds. My favorite is a size 14 or 16 orange one.*

## UV Scud (Orange)

| | |
|---|---|
| Hook: | #10-18 Tiemco 2457 |
| Thread: | Orange 6/0 Danville |
| Tail/Antennae: | Orange spooled Antron or Z-lon |
| Body: | UV shrimp pink Ice Dub |
| Shellback: | Plastic bag strip |
| Rib: | 4X mono |

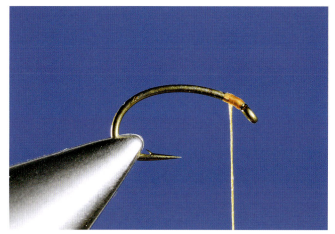

**1.** Place the hook in your vise. Attach the thread behind the hook eye.

**2.** Lay approximately 30 to 35 individual strands of orange spooled Antron on top of the hook shank at the point shown above. Make four tight wraps to hold it in place.

**3.** Leave at least ¾ inch of Antron hanging over the eye for the tail (the fly is tied backward on the hook). You will trim the tail when the fly is complete. The remaining Antron should extend over the top of the hook shank.

**4.** Tie down the remaining strand of Antron. Do not cut the extra Antron; it will be used for the antennae.

**5.** Using a rotary cutter, straight-edge, and a self-healing mat, cut a ⅛-inch strip off a Ziploc bag.

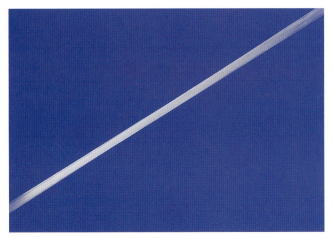

**6.** The strip should look like this.

**7.** Wrap the thread back toward the hook point. With several wraps of thread, tie in the plastic strip on the shank at a point between the hook point and the hook bend.

**8.** Tie in a piece of monofilament for the ribbing between the hook point and hook bend. This will help develop the taper near the hook bend.

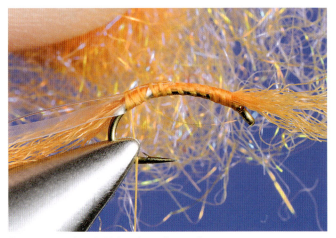

**9.** Remove the dubbing from its package.

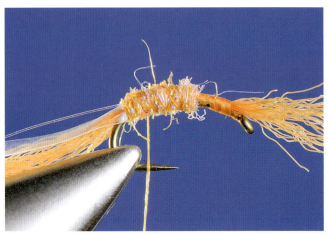

**10.** Begin developing the taper in the head area with a layer of dubbing between the hook bend and hook point. Wrap the thread back to a point above the barb.

**11.** Wrap another thin layer of dubbing between the barb and hook point.

**12.** Dub the remaining part of the abdomen and leave the thread just behind the hook eye.

**13.** Comb out the legs with a small wire brush.

**14.** The scud should look like this after you have brushed down the legs.

**15.** Pull the plastic strip over the abdomen. Secure with four tight wraps of thread behind the hook eye. Clip the plastic as close as you can to the thread. You can also tie a half hitch to keep the thread from falling off the hook eye.

**16.** Wrap the monofilament rib clockwise with six to eight turns tightly enough to sink it into the shellback.

**17.** Tie off the monofilament with four tight wraps of thread. Tie another half hitch to keep the thread from falling off the eye.

**18.** Use a bodkin to pull down any of the dubbing fibers that got trapped during the ribbing process. Be careful not to accidentally break any of the monofilament when you are pulling down the trapped legs.

**19.** Trim the dubbing parallel with the bottom of the hook. Whip-finish and clip the thread.

**20.** Trim the antennae and tail to length. The antennae should be ¾ of a hook gap, and the tail should be a hook gap long.

**21.** Using your index finger, fan the tail out. The fly should be slightly tapered from the antennae to the tail. There should be between six to eight prominent wraps of monofilament to produce a realistic looking shellback. The legs should hang down to, or just beyond, the hook point.

## UV Scud (Tan)

| | |
|---|---|
| Hook: | #10-18 Dai-Riki 135 or Tiemco 2457 |
| Thread: | Light-cahill 6/0 Uni-Thread |
| Tail/Antennae: | Tan Antron or Z-lon |
| Body: | UV light-yellow Ice Dub |
| Shellback: | Plastic bag strip |
| Rib: | 4X mono |

## UV Scud (Olive)

| | |
|---|---|
| Hook: | #10-18 Dai-Riki 135 or Tiemco 2457 |
| Thread: | Olive 6/0 Uni-Thread |
| Tail/Antennae: | Olive Antron or Z-lon |
| Body: | UV light-olive Ice Dub |
| Shellback: | Plastic bag strip |
| Rib: | 4X mono |

# CHAPTER 22

# McFlylon Mysis

*M*ysis relicta, or opossum shrimp, are native to Russia, Scandinavian countries, and northern Canada. Initially they were stocked in British Columbia's Kootney Lake, and the growth rates of the kokanee salmon increased immensely, which prompted other game and fish agencies in 1949 to introduce *Mysis* shrimp into other kokanee lakes.

Colorado Division of Wildlife (CDOW) began experimenting with *Mysis* shrimp by dumping them into Dillon, Taylor Park, and Ruedi reservoirs in the early 1970s to try to fatten up kokanee salmon that lived in the shallow bays, coves, and inlets. The jury was still out on whether the *Mysis* shrimp would produce the results that CDOW was looking for. Their strategy backfired in one sense, because *Mysis* shrimp are omnivorous

filter feeders, feeding heavily on zooplankton, which unfortunately is an important food organism for juvenile trout and young kokanee salmon.

Another interesting finding was that *Mysis* shrimp are sensitive to light and thrive in water temperatures of 57 degrees or lower. That meant the shallow bays were too warm, and the *Mysis* migrated to the deeper zones of the lake during the day. At night, they would go into the shallow water, when the temperatures were cooler. Since kokanee salmon follow exactly the opposite migratory routes, they could not take advantage of the *Mysis* shrimp.

Biologists never entertained the impact that the *Mysis* shrimp would have below the reservoirs. Many tailwaters now

*Over the years, this has been one of my best* Mysis *patterns. I first learned about this pattern from Randy Smith, who originally tied it with poly yarn rather than McFlylon. One of the key features of a* Mysis *shrimp is its dark, prominent pair of eyes.*
JAY NICHOLS

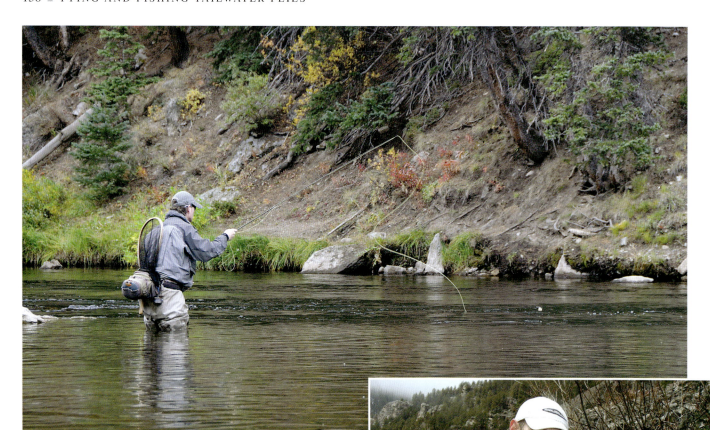

*I carry both clear and opaque* Mysis *patterns to imitate live and dead shrimp. My favorites are Laney's Mysis, McFlylon Mysis, and Will Sands' Epoxy Mysis.*

*Landon Mayer caught this huge rainbow with a* Mysis *pattern on the Taylor River. Colorado Division of Wildlife began putting* Mysis *shrimp into Taylor Park Reservoir in the early 1970s, and the tailrace below has never been the same.*

*Top: Targeting big* Mysis-*fed trout is the ultimate challenge for tailwater enthusiasts. You must have a keen eye, the right fly, and a deadly accurate presentation. The author sight-fishes to a large rainbow on the Taylor River with a McFlylon Mysis.* JAY NICHOLS

hold trophy trout that prey heavily on outflowing *Mysis* shrimp from the dam above. During runoff and seasonal lake turnover, enormous numbers of *Mysis* shrimp exit the dam. According to Will Sands at Taylor Creek Fly Shop, "The greatest concentrations of *Mysis* shrimp exit the dam during higher flows because there is greater suction near the dam face." This pulls more *Mysis* from deeper within the reservoir that would not normally get flushed out with lower flows. Trout feeding heavily on *Mysis* shrimp have brilliant colors from the high protein diet. Trout eating a steady diet of *Mysis* can easily double their weight in one year, with some fish reaching upward of 15 pounds.

Living *Mysis* shrimp are transparent within the reservoir, but they perish quickly after they hit moving water. Observant anglers will see tiny white specks (dead *Mysis*) trapped on the weed beds and algae-covered rocks. My stomach samples prove that trout key on both transparent and opaque imitations.

In Colorado, the Frying Pan, Blue, and Taylor have reliable populations of *Mysis* shrimp. Like scuds, *Mysis* shrimp are available to trout year-round, but their greatest importance is when higher flows flush the shrimp from the tailrace below. When there is a shortfall of *Mysis* exiting the dam, trout will eat midges and mayflies to fill the void.

## RIGGING AND FISHING TIPS

My *Mysis* rig changes based on the current conditions. It's not a bad idea to seine the water before you begin fishing the Taylor, Blue, or Frying Pan rivers. Even though you see dead *Mysis* trapped in the weeds, that does not prove trout are eating drifting *Mysis*. A seine will remove any doubt of whether there are any *Mysis* drifting mid-column and help you decipher what size the shrimp are. A stomach pump will also help you decipher whether the trout are eating *Mysis* that are drifting in the current.

When the flows are within their normal historic levels, I tend to fish my *Mysis* and a midge or mayfly imitation. If flows are high and heavy concentrations of *Mysis* are spurting from the dam, I fish one transparent and one opaque Mysis. From my past experiences, stomach samples show equal percentages of live (clear) and dead (opaque) shrimp, suggesting that fish eat a combination of live shrimp exiting the dam and dead shrimp dislodged from aquatic foliage.

As with all nymphing, regulating the depth at which you fish your flies is critical. On the Taylor and Frying Pan, a lot of fish are holding in front of big boulders in the middle column of the water, and good presentations to them require you to

*I like to trail a Flashback Mercury Pheasant Tail off a McFlylon Mysis or fish two* Mysis *patterns: a McFlylon Mysis and a transparent pattern such as Joe Shafer's Laney's Mysis or Will Sands' Epoxy Mysis Shrimp.*

constantly adjust your weight. You may also have to fish Mysis in shallow water. According to Will Sands, "Once *Mysis* get flushed from the dam, they try to swim toward the surface because they do not like moving water. At times, trout really key on the *Mysis* near the surface of the water and I will grease a poly *Mysis* shrimp and drop my Epoxy Mysis Shrimp off of it like a traditional dry-and-dropper rig."

## McFlylon Mysis

| | |
|---|---|
| Hook: | #16-20 Tiemco 100 |
| Thread: | White 8/0 Danville or Uni-Thread |
| Tail/Antennae: | White McFlylon |
| Body: | White ostrich herl |
| Shellback: | White McFlylon |
| Eyes: | Black Hareline Micro Tubing |

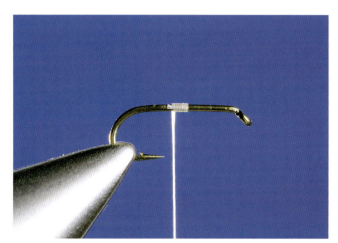

**1.** Place the hook in your vise and attach the thread at the midpoint of the hook shank.

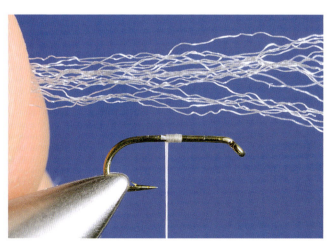

**2.** Clip one strand from the main bundle of McFlylon and divide it into thirds (about 20 to 25 fibers).

**3.** At the midpoint, attach one of the divided portions of McFlylon with four tight wraps of thread. Wrap the thread back to a point on the shank above the barb.

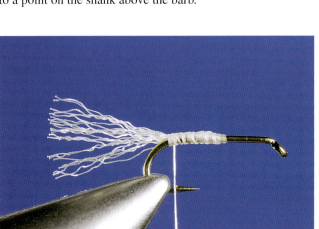

**4.** Clip the McFlylon tail so that it is the length of the hook shank. Wrap a uniform thread base over it and return the thread to the tie-in point above the barb.

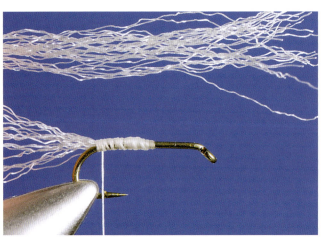

**5.** Grab another divided strand of McFlylon (20 to 25 fibers) with your index finger and thumb. This clump of McFlylon will form the shellback.

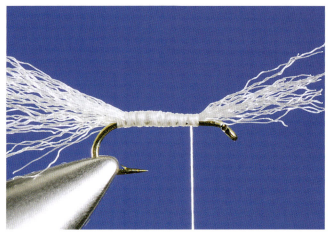

**6.** Place the McFlylon strand on top of the hook shank and secure it with several wraps of thread.

**7.** Clip the extra McFlylon that protrudes beyond the hook eye. Bury the butt ends and smooth out the thread base.

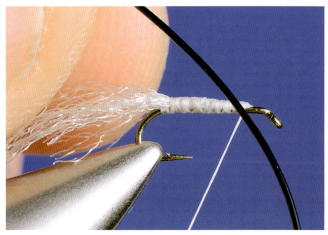

**8.** Lay a piece of black Hareline Micro Tubing across the hook shank at the point shown above.

**9.** Secure the tubing with three diagonal wraps of thread from the back side of the thread base to the front of the tubing. Create an X pattern by making another three diagonal wraps from the front of the tubing to the back of the tubing. Leave the thread hanging behind the tubing.

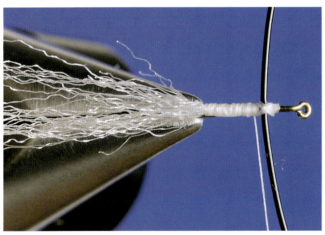

**10.** Top view of the tubing tied in perpendicular to the hook.

**11.** Wrap the thread back toward the hook bend, leaving the thread hanging above the barb.

**12.** Tie in two full pieces of ostrich herl by the tips with four tight wraps of thread.

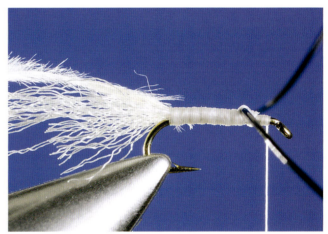

**13.** Wrap the thread forward, leaving it in front of the Micro Tubing.

**14.** Palmer the ostrich herl forward and tie it off just behind the hook eye.

**15.** Clip the butt ends of the ostrich herl and secure it with four tight wraps of thread.

**16.** Pull the MyFlylon up and over the palmered ostrich herl and Micro Tubing and tie it off just behind the hook eye with four tight wraps.

**17.** Hold the McFlylon upright and trim any remaining fibers.

**18.** Pull the Micro Tubing back with your index finger and thumb and make four tight wraps of thread to clean up the head.

**19.** Whip-finish and clip the thread. If you need to, pull back any Micro Tubing that is in your way.

**20.** Trim the eyes as close as you can without cutting the ostrich herl. The eyes are one of the most important aspects of this fly.

# CHAPTER 23

# Limeade

From the bottom of the river to the top, matching the hatch is a problem-solving exercise that requires careful observation and a thorough understanding of the correlation between the "natural" and the artificial fly used to imitate it. At other times, however, "unmatching the hatch" can be an effective strategy, too. By thinking outside the box and fishing with big, gaudy, or brightly colored flies, you can often entice fish to strike when they otherwise would not.

On many tailwaters you'll need a good attractor dry fly in the summer after flows become stable and trout get accustomed to eating a variety of foods, such as caddis, mayflies, and stoneflies, on the surface of the water. One of my favorite tactics at this time—whether I'm guiding clients or enjoying a personal day of fishing—is to "pound fish up" with dry flies when nothing is hatching.

Some of my most memorable days on a trout stream have been when I fished attractor dry flies with my father in the Gunnison Valley. I can't even begin to tell you how many fish we have caught over the years with Humpies, Royal Wulffs, H&L Variants, Renegades, and Limeades during the summer on the East, Taylor, and Gunnison rivers. All three rivers are known for their selective trout and excellent hatches of mayflies, stoneflies, and caddisflies. Closer to home, I have had 30-plus-fish days fishing attractors on the Blue in late July and early August. While matching the hatch can be one of the most satisfying parts of fly fishing, successfully unmatching it is fulfilling, too.

*The Limeade is one of my favorite attractor dry flies. It floats high and is easy to see.* JAY NICHOLS

*I use this pattern on my local tailwaters, but it also travels well. Here, Keith Lang and Jeff Mavelli cast attractor dry flies on the Mitchell River in British Columbia. Large rainbows will often feed on attractor dry flies opportunistically if they have been accustomed to seeing a lot of adult insects fluttering near the surface.*

If the fish have been feeding on sporadic-to-heavy hatches of caddis, mayflies, stoneflies, and terrestrials, the chances are pretty good that you can entice a trout to eat a big, juicy dry fly. Big trout are opportunistic feeders and rarely refuse the chance to capitalize on an easy meal. Fishing attractors can also be effective during a heavy hatch when the surface is blanketed with naturals. I have witnessed several occasions on the San Juan River where there were two dozen Blue-Winged Olives in

a square foot of surface area in the Texas Hole. Trout were rising everywhere, but they were extremely difficult to fool—my artificial imitation was one of 25 mayfly duns in that square foot from which the trout had to choose. I have experienced similar situations with caddisflies on the Arkansas River near Salida, Colorado, and the South Platte near Deckers. If you have fished the Mother's Day Caddis hatch, you'll know exactly what I'm talking about. In these cases, matching the

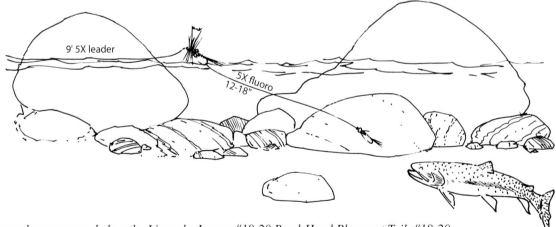

*If I fish a nymph or emerger below the Limeade, I use a #18-20 Bead-Head Pheasant Tail, #18-20 Bead-Head Barr Emerger, #18-20 Mighty Mite Baetis, or a #20-22 Zebra Midge. Cover the water methodically, paying close attention for any flashes below the Limeade. You will get plenty of strikes on the Limeade, which makes this approach effective, especially in shallow water where traditional nymphs rigs tend to get hung up.*

hatch may actually be a bad idea even though the trout are feeding heavily and selectively on adult caddis. Often, during a dense hatch, the fish are better able to distinguish a larger, brighter fly from the rest of the naturals, and because the fly stands out, they may be attracted to it. You also stand a better chance of seeing a fly that is one to two times larger than the naturals during a blanket hatch.

The Limeade, a variation of Lee Wulff's hairwing patterns, has been one of my go-to attractor patterns for the past several years. The Limeade floats high on fast, riffled water; it's durable; and—most importantly—the bright chartreuse wings make it easy to see. In fact, I invented the Limeade because I was tired of trying to see my attractor dry fly in the harsh evening glare.

Though it is primarily an attractor, I do use it to match the hatch. With its mayfly silhouette, a #12 Limeade fishes remarkably well during Green Drake hatches. Bushy hackle and stiff moose-hair tails help it ride high on rough water, precisely where Green Drakes commonly emerge. I have fooled countless trout on the North Fork of the South Platte with this fly during Green Drake hatches.

I have included other hair-wing patterns in this chapter such as the Cherry Limeade, Royal Wulff, Adams Wulff, and H&L Variant. They have all been so effective for me over the years that I cannot imagine fishing a Western trout stream during the summer and autumn without them. Though some of the materials vary, the tying steps for these flies are similar to the Limeade, and you should have no trouble tying them if you master the Limeade.

## RIGGING AND FISHING TIPS

You can fish the Limeade as a single attractor dry fly, fish it above a small midge or mayfly to help you locate your smaller fly in foam or scum lines, or fish it as a dry-and-dropper rig and suspend a small nymph or emerger off the hook bend.

I most frequently fish my Limeade as a single dry fly, quartering my delivery upstream at a 45-degree angle. I dab it into small pockets and high-stick it, keeping all the fly line and leader off the water to achieve a drag-free float. Carefully manage your fly line underneath your casting hand's index finger to avoid any unnecessary slack that might result in drag or a poor hook-set. Be prepared to set the hook quickly, as fish will dart out of deeper water to grab the fly. You may also fish the Limeade with a straight upstream delivery, methodically covering the water and showing it to as many fish as possible.

Fish each seam thoroughly, and pay close attention to the glassy part of the pocket, which I like to think of as a miniature pool. I get considerably more strikes in the glassy part than in the seams on each side of the boulder. Trout also hold toward the back end of the pocket where there is often another boulder that slows down the current, producing a slick that is an especially good place to fish dry flies.

When you fish pocketwater, especially when flows are still on the high side, be careful on the slick, algae-coated boulders. Many anglers avoid fishing quick, boulder-strewn sections of a trout stream because it's difficult to negotiate, but targeting pocketwater is a good option if you want to avoid crowds and reach less-pressured trout. I use a wading staff and cleated soles on my boots to help me navigate areas that are tough to wade.

*Sometimes fishing a large attractor will entice a trout to eat your fly when the surface of the river is covered with huge numbers of naturals.* JAY NICHOLS

### *Limeade*

| | |
|---|---|
| Hook: | #10-18 Tiemco 100 |
| Thread: | Black 8/0 Uni-Thread |
| Tail: | Moose body hair |
| Abdomen: | Green Flashabou with peacock herl |
| Wing: | Chartreuse calf tail |
| Hackle: | Brown rooster |

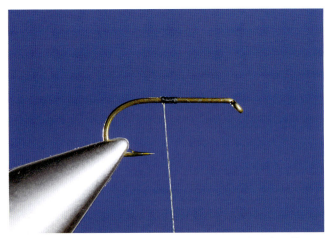

**1.** Place the hook in the vise, attach the thread at the 40 percent point on the hook shank, and clip the tag end.

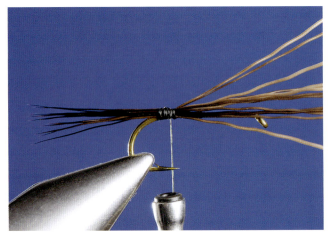

**2.** Cut 12 to 14 hairs from a patch of moose hide. Remove the underfur and stack them. Lay the hair on top of the hook shank and tie them in just before the bend with several wraps that have increasing pressure to prevent flaring. The tail should be the length of the hook shank.

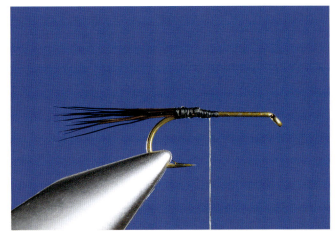

**3.** Clip the butts and cover them with thread.

**4.** Cut a clump of chartreuse calf hair, remove the underfur, and stack it. The wing should be as long as the hook shank. With your material hand's index finger and thumb, place the calf hair on top of the hook shank and make two loose turns with the thread to hold the calf hair in position.

**5.** Slowly tighten the thread wraps by pulling the thread straight down. Continue holding the calf hair with your thumb and index finger as you secure the wing with several wraps of thread.

**6.** Lift the butt ends of the calf hair with your material hand's index finger and thumb and clip them. Wrap thread over the butts to create a relatively smooth underbody.

**7.** Pull back the calf-tail fibers and build a thread wedge in front of the wing to prop it up. Pack the thread wraps as close and tight to the base of the wings as you can, striving for a smooth taper in front of the wing.

**8.** Divide the calf hair into two equal clumps. Make five cross wraps from the back of the wing to the front of the wing and then five wraps from the front to the back.

**9.** Post the wing farthest from you by making several clock-wise wraps of thread around the base of the wing.

**10.** Anchor your posting wraps by taking two tight wraps of thread behind the wings. The posted wing should be perpendicular to the hook shank.

**11.** Post the wing closest to you by making several clockwise wraps of thread around the base of the wing. Take two tight wraps of thread behind the wings to lock them in place. Put a drop of Doug's Head Cement on the base of each wing.

**12.** Smooth out any uneven spots on the underbody and wrap the thread back to above the barb.

**15.** Select two full pieces of peacock herl from an eye and tie them in by the tips just in front of the Flashabou.

**13.** Tie in two strands of green Flashabou and wrap the thread forward so that it is above the hook point.

**16.** Wrap the herl forward and tie them off. The peacock herl should be the same width as the Flashabou.

**14.** Wrap the Flashabou forward and tie it off. Make sure the Flashabou is tight and covers the black thread. Trim the Flashabou and cover the ends with thread. The width of the Flashabou band should be about 20 percent of the hook shank.

**17.** Clip the butt ends of the peacock herl and cover with thread.

**18.** Select and size a brown rooster hackle so that when flared, it is approximately 1¼ to 1½ times the hook gap. Strip the barbules off the hackle and lay it on top of the hook shank behind the wings with the dull side facing up. The exposed quill should be about the length of half the hook shank and extend slightly beyond the wings. Secure the hackle in front of the peacock and wrap the thread forward to the wings.

**19.** Wrap the thread in front of the wings, over the butt end of the hackle quill, and secure it with two tight wraps. Smooth out the taper between the wings and the hook eye, and leave the thread just behind the hook eye.

**20.** Wrap the hackle from the front edge of the peacock to the back edge of the wings. Pull the wings back, and continue wrapping the hackle forward to just short of the hook eye. Make sure the first turn of hackle in front of the wing is right in front of the wing. Tie off the hackle, whip-finish, and cement the head.

*Cherry Limeade*

| | |
|---|---|
| Hook: | #10-18 Tiemco 100 |
| Thread: | Black 8/0 Uni-Thread |
| Tail: | Moose body hair |
| Abdomen: | Red Flashabou with peacock herl |
| Wing: | Pink calf hair |
| Hackle: | Brown rooster |

### H&L Variant

Hook:       #12-18 Tiemco 100
Thread:     Black 8/0 Uni-Thread
Tail:       White calf tail or body hair
Abdomen:    Stripped peacock quill and peacock herl
Wing:       White calf tail or body hair
Hackle:     Brown rooster

### Adams Wulff

Hook:       #12-18 Tiemco 100
Thread:     Black 8/0 Uni-Thread
Tail:       Brown and grizzly hackle, mixed
Abdomen:    Adams gray Superfine
Wing:       Calf tail or body hair
Hackle:     Brown and grizzly rooster

### Royal Wulff

Hook:       #12-18 Tiemco 100
Thread:     Black 8/0 Uni-Thread
Tail:       Moose body hair
Abdomen:    Peacock and red floss
Wing:       Calf tail or body hair
Hackle:     Brown rooster

# CHAPTER 24

# *Renegade*

The Renegade was developed in 1928 by Taylor "Bear-tracks" Williams. Williams cranked out his first Renegade one afternoon in his Sawtooth Shack fly shop in Gooding, Idaho, in preparation for the evening hatch on the Malad River. In the late 1930s, Williams became the head guide at the Sun Valley Lodge and a regular fishing and hunting companion of Ernest Hemingway. According to Hemingway, "He [Williams] was an excellent dry-fly fisherman." Hemingway believed that the Renegade was a good egg-laying caddis imitation.

The fore-and-aft hackling style, which was developed centuries before the birth of Williams' concoction, allows the Renegade to float much higher than a standard dry fly. Additionally, the white hackle at the front of the fly makes it highly visible even in fast, choppy water. Selecting quality hackle for the Renegade is very important. Many dry flies have foam bodies, elk- or deer-hair wings, CDC, or a stiff tail to help support the fly and assist in floatation. This is not the case with the Renegade. It relies strictly on the hackle to keep it afloat on riffled waters. I typically use the Whiting Farms 100 packs. Because they are pre-sized, you can tie consistent flies without having to use a hackle gauge. Simply match the hackle with the appropriate hook size and you're ready to go. The 100 packs are available in sizes 8 through 24, and there

*I appreciate the Renegade for its simplicity. My father introduced me to this fly 35 years ago on one of our regular visits to the Gunnison River.* JAY NICHOLS

171

*Jim Dorsey hooked nearly a dozen fish with an attractor in this beautiful run. My father is a passionate dry-fly angler, and the Renegade has always been his favorite fly.*

are many colors to choose from. The most popular are cream, dun, grizzly, and brown. Whiting Farms guarantees that you will get at least 100 flies per pack, which makes their hackle a great value.

According to Bruce Staples, an Idaho Falls author, historian, and master fly tier, "Williams could not have chosen a better material than peacock herl to form the body. It remains, in this age of hi-tech synthetics, a consummate attractor of fish." Marv Taylor, a Boise author, columnist, and fly-tying innovator agrees: "The Renegade has probably caught more fish in Idaho than any other dry-fly pattern." Personally, I believe the iridescent sheen of peacock herl works magic on trout. It's not coincidental that patterns like the Halfback, Prince, Pheasant Tail, Royal Wulff, and H&L Variant, to name only a few, are some of the best trout producers of all time. They all have one thing in common—peacock herl.

I typically use peacock eyes, not strung peacock herl, to create a fluffy abdomen. After a few fish, the peacock may start to fall apart. You can replace the ragged fly with a new one, since they are so easy to tie, or keep on fishing it. My dad swears that a Renegade fishes better once it becomes worn and tattered. I have watched him catch fish after fish with a Renegade that had the hackle and peacock herl dangling from it. Another option is to reverse rib a piece of wire or 6X tippet through the peacock before tying in the final hackle near the

hook eye. This ensures that the fly will not come apart. I dress the hackle with Loon Aquel and avoid putting floatant on the peacock herl because it mats downs the fibers.

While working on this book, I have reflected on my 30 years of fly tying—I actually dug up some of my old fly boxes from 25 years ago. There have been so many advancements in tying materials, hooks, vises, and tools in an effort to improve techniques and create innovative fly patterns. Hard-fished, selective trout have led many of today's innovators to tie more realistic patterns than ever. Fly fishing has become as much of an art as a popular pastime or sport. Many of today's creative and cutting-edge patterns catch as many fishermen as they do fish, but one must remember that the tried-and-true patterns of yesteryear like the Hare's Ear, standard Adams, and Renegade still catch as many fish now as they did 50 years ago.

I believe that trout get conditioned to seeing the same fly over and over again and become fly-wise. That's what makes the Renegade so special. It's an oldie but goodie that doesn't get all the hype and publicity that a lot of other flies get. My guess is that the average angler doesn't even carry a Renegade in his or her fly boxes anymore. Sometimes anglers have a tendency to outthink themselves with all the modern advancements and ever-present urge to create the ultimate fly. Even though I love to create new patterns, my recommendation is that you remain open-minded, experiment with your flies and tactics, and never rule out traditional patterns and techniques developed by our forefathers.

## RIGGING AND FISHING TIPS

Sometimes using an attractor pattern like a Renegade will draw attention to your fly. As Mike Lawson wrote in *Spring Creeks:* "When the surface is blanketed with tiny mayflies, matching the hatch can really be a handicap. You must do better than match the hatch. If there are forty-nine tiny mayflies per square foot of surface area, and you've matched the hatch perfectly, you just created fifty mayflies per square foot of surface area." Lawson believes that when a trout gets into a selective feeding pattern, it will rarely rise more than once as two or three feet of water passes overhead. That means a trout will let dozens of naturals drift past between each rise.

This may be why the Renegade fishes remarkably well during a caddis hatch. While fishing a Renegade during a full-blown caddis hatch tends to go a little against the grain, it works. It's hard to argue with success. You can fish the Renegade during the peak of caddis season (late April through mid June) or when the caddis are hatching sporadically in mid to late summer (mid July through September).

I often use a larger attractor or a brightly colored dry fly as an indicator fly so that I can see my smaller fly. If there is a blanket hatch, and you are adamant about matching the hatch but are having difficulty seeing your adult caddis on the water, consider attaching a #16 Elk-Hair, Goddard, or Puterbaugh Caddis on 14 to 16 inches of tippet tied to the bend of a #14 Renegade.

The Renegade is also effective fished as a wet fly on the swing during a caddis hatch. Cast downstream at a 45-degree angle and let your flies swing until they are below you. Take a step or two downriver and repeat this process, covering the river methodically. The strikes will be obvious—the leader will tighten or you will feel an aggressive tug. I typically place one or two #4 split-shot 12 inches above the fly.

At times, a Renegade doubles as a midge cluster or a single midge in smaller sizes. A #18-22 Renegade shares many similarities with the Griffith's Gnat. In sizes 12 through 16 it can be fished as a midge cluster. I have fooled trout in Cheesman Canyon during a midge hatch with a #20 Renegade.

Most of the time, I just use the Renegade as an attractor. I prefer to fish the Renegade as a single dry fly on a 9-foot leader tapering to 5X tippet. For me, casting a single dry fly is the heart and soul of our sport. Fishing with an attractor dry fly is graceful and relaxing. When I fish with an attractor, I don't have to worry about matching the hatch, changing flies, or adjusting my weight or strike indicator depth. I think it fishes best when there is no hatch at all or there are a few mayflies or caddis buzzing around the river. Typically when the Pale Morning Dun and Green Drake hatches fizzle out for the season, there is a lull in the afternoon mayfly activity until the Blue-Winged Olives start hatching in September. Due to the lull in the hatches, I believe the fish are looking for food. Fish all the likely spots, such as pocketwater, riffles, runs, and pools. Don't be afraid to fish skinny areas such as bank water and shallow riffles, transitional zones (mid-channel shelves and gravel bars), and back channels. I have watched in amazement as my dad fooled 12- to 16-inch trout in skinny water in back channel or braided sections of a stream that many anglers overlook.

*Rainbow trout take a Renegade with confidence. Renegade connoisseurs have always considered this beautiful little dry fly to be the ultimate pattern for catching cutthroat and rainbows.*

## Renegade

| | |
|---|---|
| Hook: | #12-22 Tiemco 100 |
| Thread: | Black 8/0 Uni-Thread |
| Hackle: | Brown rooster |
| Abdomen: | Peacock |
| Rib (optional): | Monofilament |
| Hackle: | White rooster |

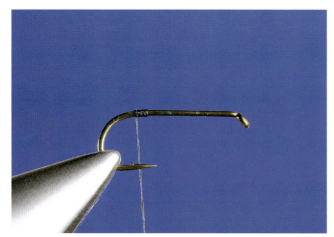

**1.** Place the hook in your vise and attach the thread at the hook bend.

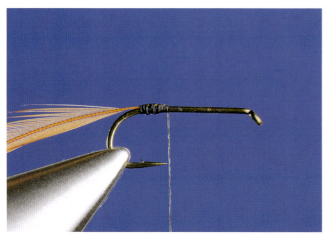

**2.** Select and size a brown saddle hackle. The fibers should be 1½ times the width of the hook gap. Strip a hook gap's worth of barbules from the stem, and tie it in as shown, with the dull side of the feather facing up.

**3.** Wrap the hackle forward four to six turns. The rear hackle should cover about a quarter of the hook shank. Hold the hackle tight with your tying hand and make four tight wraps of thread with your other hand to secure the feather.

**4.** Clip the top of the feather and any stray hackle. Take two more wraps of thread over the clipped stem.

**5.** Wrap a smooth thread base to the point shown above and back to a point just in front of the rear hackle.

**6.** Select two pieces of fluffy peacock herl from the eye. Tie them in tip first, as shown. Wrap the thread forward to the point shown above.

**7.** Wrap the two pieces of peacock herl forward and tie them off with four tight wraps of thread. Each wrap of peacock herl should be in front of the previous wrap to avoid matting down the herl.

**8.** Clip the herl tips and take four tight wraps of thread.

**9.** Select and size a cream saddle hackle. It should be the same size as the rear hackle. Strip a hook gap's worth of barbules from the stem and tie the hackle in with the dull side facing up. Leave the thread behind the hook eye.

**10.** Wrap the cream hackle forward with the same number of turns you used with the rear hackle (four to six). Tie off the cream hackle, clip the tip of the feather, and remove any stray fibers. Make four tight wraps of thread to cover the butt end of the stem and clean up the head.

**11.** Whip-finish and clip the thread.

# Organizing Your Tailwater Boxes

If you're fumbling through plastic cups or a hodgepodge of unorganized fly boxes, you aren't fishing. Over the years, I have refined, through trial and error, my method for organizing my fly boxes. My goals include simplicity, neatness, carrying only the essentials, and keeping them organized so that I can find them quickly. If you have the right fly, but cannot locate it, it really defeats the purpose.

There are many excellent fly boxes on the market to help you organize your flies. My favorites include Richard Wheatley (swing leaf and ripple foam), Myran, C&F Design, and plastic ripple-foam varieties. They each have their own advan-tages to help you organize your flies. These are by no means the only fly boxes that you should consider. They have worked well for me, but don't be afraid to experiment and find out what works best for you. Before you buy a box, consider your budget, the box's size and storage capability, how it functions, and personal appeal. I am a firm believer in getting what you pay for; therefore, I tend to shy away from cheap fly boxes.

I use the Richard Wheatley swing-leaf boxes ($3\frac{1}{2}$ x $2\frac{3}{8}$ x 1 inch and 6 x $3\frac{1}{2}$ x $1\frac{1}{2}$ inch) for my small nymphs (#18-26). For my bigger nymphs (#10-18), I use their ripple-foam fly boxes. The ripple-foam boxes are ideal for caddis larvae and

*Having the right fly when you need it is critical to success.* JAY NICHOLS

bead-head nymphs, especially those with hackled collars. I organize my flies by category so that I only have to take the boxes that I need on each outing.

Wheatley fly boxes are the best money can buy. They lend a little class to the sport and prove you're serious about fly selection. The swing-leaf boxes start at about $40. Don't let the cost of the fly box fool you—I have had many of my Wheatley boxes for over 15 years. The fly box itself is indestructible. You can purchase replacement foam inserts for a nominal cost. One of the advantages to the Wheatley swing leaf is that, in effect, you have two fly boxes in one, which allows you to carry thousands of flies in a single box. I can neatly organize up to 50 nymphs in a single row.

I use Myran clear plastic fly boxes with 6, 12, and 18 compartments for holding my dry flies. By cramming your dry flies into a ripple-foam fly box, you risk mashing down the hackle underside of your dry fly, causing it to sink at the most inopportune time. One of the many benefits to the Myran boxes is that they are lightweight and take up very little space in your vest or chest pack. They are extremely durable and are easy to open and close with their nifty little brass pin hinge system. In addition, they are reasonably priced—starting at $4.95. If for some reason you do crack one, they are easily replaced. I typically get several seasons out of one box.

Another advantage to the Myran fly box is that you can easily see the contents. I organize my boxes by category or by hatch to simplify things on the stream. For example, I keep all my midge, Blue-Winged Olive, Pale Morning Dun, Red Quill, Green Drake, Trico, caddisfly, and stonefly imitations in their own separate fly box. I also use a Myran fly box for my egg patterns. Label your fly boxes to make things easier on the stream.

I use the C&F Design boxes for streamers, stoneflies, crane-fly larvae, and leech patterns. The boxes work well because the slits in the foam minimize the wear and tear on your fly box when taking flies out and putting them back in. This can be a big problem with larger flies, because the hook and barb point is naturally larger. There are many different models to choose from—8-, 10- and 14-row designs as well as flip-page models, which are very popular for tailwater enthusiasts. The flip-page models are similar to Wheatley fly boxes. Waterproof models provide a distinct advantage if you are an aggressive wader.

In a small (4 x 3 x 1 inch) ripple-foam fly box, I fit more than 250 San Juan Worms in several colors and sizes. Plastic ripple-foam fly boxes are lightweight and fit into a chest pack or vest with ease. They are reasonably priced, starting around $10.00. If you wear the foam out, you can replace the fly box or purchase replacement foam inserts.

I keep all my flies boxes stored in a waterproof boat bag and only take the ones I need to match the prevailing hatches. This helps to reduce any unnecessary bulk in the vest or chest pack that can result in neck or back pain. It also reduces the risk of losing fly boxes. I generally carry my Wheatley boxes with me year-round because they are the bread and butter of my fly selection.

I also carry a Day's Worth (Cliff Outdoors) box from time to time so that I can cherry-pick a few flies from my main fly boxes. This is a beautiful small plastic magnetic box (without compartments), which allows me to carry a couple flies—be they stoneflies, crane flies, streamers, Chamois Leeches, or large dry flies like Amy's Ant—when I hike into remote areas. It conveniently fits into your shirt pocket or you chest pack or vest. This greatly reduces any bulk in your waist pack, vest, or backpack, but still allows you to cover your bases. If you do not have a Cliff box, you need to get one—they are invaluable for situations like this.

While I tie the majority of my flies, I still purchase several flies each season. I typically purchase a few flies when I travel to other states like Wyoming, Montana, Utah, or New Mexico. Prior to fishing, I try to make it a point to visit a local fly shop for up-to-date fishing information. It is always a good idea to buy a few of the hot flies if the sales associate is willing to lend their expertise on their local waters. I bought my first Barr's Tungstones and Sloan's Mighty Mite Baetis in Bozeman, Montana, prior to fishing the Madison River several years ago. I had never heard of either pattern, but today they are among my favorites. I carry several dozen of each because they have proven to be excellent producers on my local waters.

As a general rule, never purchase one or two of a specific pattern—buy at least six. I generally buy at least half a dozen of the hot flies if I do not already have them. Make it a point to keep at least one for a sample so that you can tie more. I typically take my fly-tying kit with me on my multi-day excursions to fill in any holes from excessive fly loss. Running out of a productive fly can ruin your day. I follow the same guidelines when I tie my own flies too. I generally tie at least six of each fly with the same goals in mind.

# Large Tailwater (Midges and Mayflies)

This Wheatley swing-leaf box contains a wide assortment of tiny midge and mayfly imitations and is my go-to guide box. I carry it with me year-round, regardless of the season or conditions. On the left side, **row 1** holds Bead-Head Barr Emergers (#20-22); **row 2**, Smith's Tyvek Baetis (#20-22) and a variety of Mercer's Micro Mayfly Nymphs; **row 3** contains Stalcup's Baetis (#20-22), Mercer's Epoxy PMDs (#18), and Mercer's Gold Bead Micro Stonefly Nymphs; **row 4**, more Smith's Tyvek Baetis (#22), Dorsey's Mercury Flashback RS2s (#20-22), brown Foam-Wing Baetis Emergers (#20-22), and Dorsey's Mercury Baetis (#18-20); **row 5**, more Dorsey's Mercury Baetis (#20-22), Craven's Juju Baetis (#20), and Stout's WD 50s; **row 6**, more Stalcup's Baetis (#18) and Sloan's Mighty Mite Baetis (#16-20); **row 7** has a few Stalcup's Baetis (#18), but **row 7 and 8** are predominantly filled with Dorsey's Mercury Flashback Pheasant Tails (#18-22); **rows 9 through 12** have variations of the RS2— Churchill's Sparkle Wing RS2s, Dorsey's Mercury RS2s, Dorsey's Mercury Flashback RS2s, and Mercury Sparkle Wing RS2s— and a few Mathews' Crystal Serendipities (#20) in **row 9**.

On the right side, **row 1** contains bead-head Blood Midges (#18-20); **row 2**, assorted midge emergers (#20-22) and Dorsey's Medallion Midges (#20-22); **row 3**, Dorsey's Flashback Mercury Black Beauties (#22) and Periwinkles (#18-22); **row 4**, Zebra Midge variations (#20-22) and UFO Midges (#20); **row 5**, Dorsey's Mercury Brassies (#20) and Chan's Frostbite Midges (#20); **row 6**, Craven's Poison Tungs (#18-20) and Jujubee Midges (#20-22); **row 7**, Gomez's Desert Storms (#20) and Barr's Pure Midge Larvae (#20); **row 8**, Dorsey's Mercury Black Beauties (#18-22); **row 9**, Parrott's Little Purple Midges (#20) and Dye's Pearl Jams (#20-22); **row 10**, Dorsey's Mercury Midges (#20-24); **row 11**, Dorsey's Mercury Flashback Brown Beauties and Black Beauties (#20-22) and pearl Egan's Rainbow Warriors (#20-22); **row 12**, red and black Egan's Rainbow Warriors (#20); **row 13**, a variety of tiny midge larvae and pupae (#20-24); **row 14**, some small Flashback Baetis (#24) and Dorsey's Top Secret Midges (#20-26); **row 15**, Dorsey's Mercury Blood Midges (#18-22).

# Large Tailwater (Assorted)

This is the other half of my Wheatley swing-leaf box, crammed with tiny mayfly nymphs (*Baetis*, PMDs, and Tricos), scuds, *Mysis* shrimp, caddis nymphs, and attractors. On the top left, **row 1** includes tungsten gold-bead Breadcrusts (#12-16); **row 2**, tungsten gold-bead Flashback Pheasant Tails (#16-18); **row 3** has Purple Princes (#14-18), some with copper beads and some with brass beads; **row 4**, red Dorsey's Mercury Flashback Pheasant Tails (#16-20); **row 5**, red Copper Johns (#14-16); **row 6**, McLellan's Hunchback Scuds (#14-16) and Dorsey's UV Scuds (#14-16); **row 7**, Dorsey's Mercury Cased Caddis (#18); **row 8**, several sizes of Tygart's bead-head and standard Hydropsyche; **row 9**, gold-bead Flashback Pheasant Tails (#16-18); **row 10**, Buckskins and gold-bead Buckskins (#18-20).

On the right side, **rows 1 and 2** have different varieties of PMD Barr Emergers (#16-18); **row 3**, Mercer's tungsten Micro Mayfly Nymphs (#18-22); **row 4**, olive Churchill's Sparkle Wing RS2s (#20-22); **row 5**, Dorsey's Mercury Flashback Baetis, flashback and standard BWO Barr Emergers, and olive Churchill's Sparkle Wing RS2s (#18-22); **row 6**, Dorsey's Mercury Flashback RS2s, Chung's original RS2s, and Juju Baetis (#18-22); **row 7**, Mercury Flashback RS2s, Sloan's Mighty Mite Baetis, and black Dorsey's Mercury Pheasant Tails (#20-22); **row 8**, Dorsey's Mercury Baetis and black Copper Johns (#20); **row 9**, olive Heng's BLMs, Dye's PMDs, Dorsey's Mercury PMDs, and PMD Barr Emergers (#16-18); **rows 10 and 11** have a variety of *Mysis* shrimp—Sands', Thomas', and Laney's Mysis.

# Small Tailwater (Assorted)

This is another one of my tailwater nymph boxes that I carry all the time when guiding. On the left side, **rows 1 through 3** contain a variety of sow bugs (#14-16), **row 4**, scuds, sow bugs, and soft-hackle bead-head sow bugs (#14-16); **rows 5 and 6**, variations of olive, tan, and orange scuds (#14-20); **rows 7 and 8**, Blood Worms and Dorsey's Mercury Blood Midges (#18-20); **row 9**, red San Juan Worms. On the right side, **row 1 and 2** contain Dorsey's Mercury Midges (#18-22); **row 3**, Mathews' Crystal Serendipities (#20); **row 4**, brown and gray Churchill's Sparkle Wing RS2s (#24); **row 5**, Dorsey's Top Secret Midges (#18-26); **row 6**, Dorsey's Mercury Black Beauties (#18-20); **row 7**, Dorsey's Bead-Head Midge Larva (#18); **row 8**, red thread midges (#20-22); **row 9**, Craven's Jujubee Midges (#20); **row 10**, cream Barr's Pure Midge Larvae (#20); **row 11**, poly-wing RS2s (#24); **row 12**, Chan's Frostbite Midges (#20); **row 13**, black Garcia's Rojo Midges (#20); **row 14**, Dorsey's Black Beauties (#20-22).

This half of my tailwater box includes a variety of my Mercury Nymphs. On the left side, **rows 1 through 3** contain red, black, and blue Dorsey's Mercury Brassies (#18-20); **row 4**, Dorsey's Mercury Buckskins (#18-20); **rows 5 through 7**, Dorsey's Mercury Flashback Pheasant Tails (#18-22); **rows 8 and 9**, Dorsey's Mercury Pheasant Tails (#18-20); **row 10**, Dorsey's Mercury Cased Caddis (#16-18). On the right side, **row 1** holds Baetis Foam-Wing Emergers (#20); **row 2**, copper Dorsey's Mercury Brassies (#20-22); **row 3**, Dorsey's Mercury RS2s (#18-22); **rows 4 and 5**, Dorsey's Mercury PMDs (#16-18); **rows 6 through 8**, Dorsey's Mercury Baetis (#18-22); **row 9**, Mercury Grems' Caddis Larvae (#14-16); and **row 10**, Dorsey's Mercury Cased Caddis (#14-16).

# Bead-Head and Large Nymph

This swing-leaf Wheatley is my bead-head and large nymph box. On the left, **row 1** includes tungsten-bead Prince Nymphs (#12-14, with .020 lead wire on the shanks); **rows 2 through 6** hold gold-bead Prince Nymphs (#12-18); **row 7**, tungsten-bead Flashback Pheasant Tails (#16) and tungsten-bead Mercury Pheasant Tails; **row 8**, tungsten-bead Tygart's Hydropsyches (#12-14) and LaFontaine's Sparkle Pupae (#14-16); **row 9**, olive and tan Stalcup's Bead-Head Diving Caddis (#14-16). On the right side, **row 1** includes Hare's-Ear Nymphs (#18-20); **row 2**, Bead-Head Hare's-Ear Nymphs (#14-18); **row 3**, variations of olive and natural Hare's-Ear Nymphs (#14-18); **row 4**, Bead-Head Hare's-Ear Nymphs with wing cases (#14); **row 5**, tungsten-bead Breadcrusts (#16), tungsten-bead Buckskins (#16), and tungsten-bead Hare's-Ear Nymphs (#14-16); **rows 6 through 9**, gold-bead Breadcrusts (#12-18).

# Bead-Head and Large Nymph

This is the other half of my bead-head and large nymph box. Starting on the left, **row 1** includes tungsten-bead olive Breadcrusts (#18); **row 2**, tungsten-bead olive Breadcrusts (#16); **row 3**, bead-head olive Breadcrusts (#12-14); **row 4**, tungsten-bead Breadcrusts (#14) and standard Breadcrusts (#12-16); **row 5**, a variety of Grems' Caddis Pupa (#14-16); **row 6**, Bead-Head Buckskins (#16-18); **row 7**, Buckskins (#14-18); **rows 8 and 9**, Bead-Head Pheasant Tails, standard and flashback. On the right side, **row 1** includes Copper Johns (#16); **rows 2 and 3**, thorax bead-head mayfly nymphs (#14-16); **rows 4 through 7**, Prince Nymphs (#12-18); **row 8**, Stalcup's Bead-Head Green Drake Nymphs (#10-12).

# Stonefly

Stonefly nymphs are effective year-round on many Western waters. **Row 1** (on the left and right sides) of my stonefly box contains brown Paper Tigers (#6-8); **row 2**, brown Larva Lace woven-body stonefly nymphs (#8) and various bead-head stonefly nymphs (#6-8); **row 3**, golden Paper Tigers (#10), Parrott's Golden Stoneflies (#10), and Golden Larva Lace woven-body stoneflies (#10); **row 4**, Barr's Tungstones (#10-12) and variations of a Bitch Creek (#6-10); **row 5**, Flashback Tungstones (#10).

# Scud and Sow Bug

This is my scud and sow-bug box filled with an assortment sizes and colors. On the left side, **rows 1 and 2** include orange UV Scuds (#14-16). On the far right side of **row 2**, there are some orange Rainey's Scuds (#14). **Row 3** holds tan UV Scuds and orange Rainey's Scuds (#14); **row 4**, more orange UV Scuds (#12-14); **row 5**, light-olive UV Scuds (#14); **row 6**, tan Sow Bugs (#16). On the right side of the box, **row 1** includes dark-olive UV Scuds (#14); **row 2**, orange Stalcup's Scuds (#12-16) and McLellan's Hunchback Scuds (#14-16); **row 3**, olive Stalcup's Scuds (#12-16); **row 4**, pink and tan Sow Bugs (#16); **row 5**, flashback, bead-head, and regular versions of Rainey's Scuds; **row 6**, gray Sow Bugs (#16).

# San Juan Worm

This small ripple-foam fly box carries an assortment of San Juan Worms. I choose a color depending on the time of year, flows, and water clarity. I tend to use the brighter colors—red, orange, pink, and chartreuse—when the water is stained from spring runoff. I have fooled countless trout with a pink San Juan Worm during the peak of runoff when there was less than a foot of visibility. When spring runoff peaks and the flows begin to clear, the earthworm-brown color produces best because it resembles the natural aquatic worms that get knocked from the stream bottom during higher spates.

# Streamer

This large Scientific Anglers ripple-foam fly box includes everything from Woolly Buggers to Muddler Minnows (#6-10). This box contains standard, bead-head, cone-head, and lead-eye Woolly Buggers—some with rubber legs, which drive fish nuts—in olive, black, brown, and purple. I also carry #10 Slumpbusters, Pine Squirrel Leeches, and black Matukas.

# Blue-Winged Olive

This is one of my go-to dry-fly boxes for tailwater fishing. I carry this box with me year-round. **Row 1** contains Blue Quills (#18-22), Hi-Viz Baetis (#18-24), and Barr's Vis-a-Duns (#20-22); **row 2**, Cannon's Snow Shoe Duns (#18-22), Blue Duns (#18-22), and Blue-Winged Olives (#18-22); **row 3** includes Cannon's Snowshoe Duns (#20), Mathews' Sparkle Duns (#18-22), and Parachute Blue-Winged Olives (#20-22).

# Midge

I carry my adult midge box with me all season. This box contains a variety of adult midges: Parachute Adamses, Befus' Midges, Cannon's Snowshoe Midges, Hi-Viz Midges, Matt's Midges, Griffith's Gnats, and Cannon's Snowshoe Clusters (#20-26). My favorite midge pattern is a #26 Parachute Adams.

# Caddis

My caddis box contains several varieties and colors of adult caddis. Included in this box are variations of Elk-Hair Caddis, Goddard Caddis, Garcia's Mother's Day Caddis, Hemmingway Caddis, Kingrey's Foam Caddis, and my favorite (bottom right), Puterbaugh's Caddis (#12-18).

# Attractors

This attractor dry-fly box is filled with highly visible flies that float high on choppy Western waters. This box contains variations of Adamses, Royal Humpies, Royal Wulffs, H&L Variants, Limeades, Cherry Limeades, Quill Gordons, and Royal Coachmans (#12-18).

# Large Dry Fly

This plastic compartment dry-fly box holds my large dry flies like Amy's Ants, Rubber-Legged Stimulators (orange, yellow, and pearl), and Foamulators (orange and yellow). If I'm fishing in my drift boat, I'll take the whole box; otherwise I grab what I need and throw it in a Cliff Outdoors Day's Worth box.

# INDEX